Amazon FBA for Beginners

A Step-by-Step Guide to Build a Profitable E-Commerce Business: How to Make Money Online and Create Passive Income by Selling on Amazon

The content within this book has been derived from various sources. Please consult a licensed professional before attempting any techniques outlined in this book.

By reading this document, the reader agrees that under no circumstances is the author responsible for any losses, direct or indirect, which are incurred as a result of the use of information contained within this document, including, but not limited to, — errors, omissions, or inaccuracies.

Table of Content

6

Chapter 1: Introduction to Amazon FBA

Congratulations on purchasing *Amazon FBA for Beginners* and thank you for doing so.

What is Amazon FBA?

First, the acronym FBA stands for "Fulfillment through Amazon", an Amazon carrier that covers your orders for you. By enrolling in the FBA program, you allow Amazon to pick, pack and ship your orders. This, through the huge demand existing in the Amazon market, allows you to grow your business, get more customers on Amazon, and fulfill your orders; forgetting how big your store becomes, Amazon takes care of the entire process. By enrolling in the Amazon FBA program, your enterprise and customers will gain entry to many benefits.

Multi-Channel Supply

You can take advantage of the multi-channel achievement capabilities of the FBA program to fulfill orders from various income channels such as your e-commerce store such as Shopify Store, your eBay or your Etsy Store.

Cost-Effective Solution

It is a low-cost-low-value and easy pricing model based solely on your sales and storage. Your product elements such as its weight and dimensions will affect the rate you pay without delay. You can take advantage of Amazon's calculation of FBA prices to estimate product fees, or you can gain entry into FBA expenses and referral commissions during the use of Data Haw for thousands of products.

Sell Globally

If you are US-based, search for global customers visiting Amazon.com, browse, and search for your exportable products through the Amazon Global Selling Program, while allowing you to easily promote in Canada and Mexico.

If you are Europe-based, take advantage of Pan-European software to sell your goods in Amazon's European markets such as the United Kingdom, Germany, France, Italy, and Spain.

How to Get Started with FBA?

Now, this brings us to How to get started with FBA? It consists of four stages: setting up FBAs, developing their product listings, tailoring their products, moving them to their assigned Amazon FBA warehouse.

Set FBA

If you already have sales on an Amazon account, add FBA to your account at Vendor Central. If you do not have sales on your Amazon account, you can create one without any difficulty.

Create Your Product List

Add your merchandise to the Amazon catalog at once, either manually, import in bulk via an Excel using Amazon's provided templates, or integrate your inventory-management software program with Amazon's API in the manner of.

Prepare your Products

Prepare your goods for e-commerce transport and ensure that they are safely and securely transported to your customers' doorsteps. Amazon practices and shipping materials that you can use.

Ship your Goods to Amazon

Make your delivery plans, and ship your shipments to Amazon Success Centers. Amazon's on-line vendors can help you through the instrumentation process.

Sit and Relax

Just kidding, of course. While this complete success administration system is a magic breeze, it is simply the simple part. Now you will want to work hard to sell your products.

Chapter 2: Must Need to Know

The service offers storage, packaging, and transportation support, carrying the burden of the vendor. The application allows marketers to ship their goods to an Amazon Achievement Center, stored in place warehouses until they are sold. When an order is placed, Amazon employees prepare the product, deliver the package, and ship the product.

Benefits of Using FBA Services

Sellers can take advantage of all resources and benefits related to Amazon when they signal for fulfillment by Amazon. Contains:

Subsidized shipping charges: Because Amazon has a relationship with shipping companies, marketers will be able to pay much less in transportation using this provider than if the gadgets were being delivered from a person's account. In addition, agents can offer a certain amount of free shipping when you believe that products offered through FBA are eligible for Amazon Prime and Free Super Saver Shipping.

Multi-Channel Fulfillment:

This capability allows Amazon to substitute the item from its inventory, pack the item, and ship it to the buyer when anyone buys an item. A seller can make an item work on its own website, and, by Amazon service fulfillment, Amazon still takes care of all the heavy lifting.

FBA Fee

Amazon charges a variety of fees for FBA members;

Standard Seller Fee: When the item is sold, the seller charges about 15–18% of the product rate as the seller's fee. How to rely on a lot of products will fluctuate. Amazon says they cost 15%, although there are some hidden prices such as refunds that are no longer fully charged back, leading to a universal cost to the seller.

Storage fee, pick and pack fee, and weight-handling fee: Amazon costs the seller a rate to store all items, another rate for selecting items, and a load-based fee on an order ship.

International shipping: Amazon now offers global exports, allowing retailers to ship their inventory all over the world.

Merchant Fulfillment (FBM)

Sellers are motivated to manually evaluate storage, packaging, and distribution stock to evaluate FBA carriers to see if this is the appropriate option for them. There are many variations in exercise between fulfillment by AMAZON.

Joint Ventures

These online retailers are able to take advantage of the convenience provided by this breakthrough service. Coming to an agreement with Amazon, Amazon can automatically ship their merchandise at these 1/3 birthday party retails that they have purchased through a couple of options, compared to dealing with the entire system. Now, as an alternative to giving a business a competitive advantage, most businesses would agree that they would have to have an FBA to remain competitive. Promoting FBA has become a business venture in itself.

Countless small and medium-sized businesses reach online customers on Amazon. In 2018, third-party market agents accounted for 58% of Amazon's annual gross sales. Buyers go to markets like Amazon for one essential reason - free shipping.

For, according to UPS Pulse of Online Shoppers 2018, the 2D main purpose is free and discounted shipping to decide what to store in the marketplace.

And while free transport will probably convince the customer to shop. It is the complete delivery journey that drives a buyer to make any other purchase.

In fact, 84% of shoppers say that they did not return to a brand only after a poor delivery experience.

Recognizing this, Amazon offers its very own fulfillment program, fulfillment by Amazon (FBA) to assure sellers fast, accurate and cheap delivery to their customers.

This publish explains how the FBA works and what you should consider before becoming a member of the program. Keep in mind, this is usually not the answer for everyone!

What Is the Supply from Amazon?

To keep it simple, FBA works like this: you promote it, then Amazon ships it.

Some of Amazon's famous achievement techniques are:

- You ship your items to Amazon to be stored in their success centers.
- After Amazon receives your list, you can screen it through its monitoring system.

- The consumer orders your goods from Amazon (or any other eCommerce platform).
- Amazon packs options and sold items.

Amazon ships your items from the chosen point of view through the customer and presents tracking information to them.

They provide customer carriers and manage return for goods.

The FBA is no longer for orders deployed on Amazon.com. For all your sales channels, Amazon stores your single composites stock in its achievement features and completes orders as soon as they are placed.

As expected, Amazon spends extravagantly on the use of its services. We will go into detail about how to calculate those fees. First, we'll talk about why agents might want to use FBA.

Benefits of using Fulfillment with the help of Amazon (FBA)

The FBA provides users with the ability to develop their commercial enterprise and acquire more customers. Through free 2-day shipping, agents can raise sales and retail money. The top benefits of joining Fulfillment through Amazon are:

Discounted Shipping Rates

Shipping velocity and its charge are two important elements that influence whether a buyer decides to purchase online.

According to the NRF, 65% of customers say they charge a free shipping threshold before adding items to a shopping cart online. In addition, 39% consider two-day delivery to be free.

17

And, if you don't provide it, buyers will save elsewhere. 29% of customer's support shopping because two-day delivery is not free.

When selling on Amazon, your FBA gadgets are eligible for free shipping, which puts them at the top of product listings. Prime individuals can avail Amazon Prime free two-day delivery on your item. All Amazon.com customers can also receive free transportation on eligible orders.

With FBA, you will receive your goods in front of customers who are searching for free shipping.

FBA customers have also entered Amazon's acclaimed customer service. Your customers can contact the Customer Guide through phone or email day and night. You will know that they are not receiving customer service, and you do not have to spend hours presenting it. Instead, you can focus on managing other parts of your operation.

Return Management

When using FBA, your customers can also process returns through Amazon's online return center. This allows them to comfortably return items when needed. Now you do not have to fear about the situation of reverse logistics. Returns are often a heavy venture for on-line vendors but are critical to a common successful on-line experience.

Studies show that 60% of online customers who make at least one return or exchange per year will make 95% of any other purchase if the return visit is positive.

Keep in mind that you are charged return processing for this service.

Using Amazon other than FBA

The FBA is not just for gadgets sold on Amazon. You can also use FBA for your personal eCommerce site. Your customers can enjoy flexible transportation preferences such as one-day, two-day, and preferred shipping times.

Achieving success in one type of channel can be difficult and expensive. Letting Amazon manage it ensures that you can give customers a great ride. Whether you are already promoting on Amazon or not, you can regularly grab your order and mode of transport across your channels.

Customer Experience

Overall, FBA can greatly improve your customer experience. You will win them with the help of providing more than one delivery option, quick transportation, as promised, an easy return process and a true patron provider from Amazon.

Seeing the "Fulfillment by Amazon" logo next to your item can go a long way with customers. You can increase your income and present a regular buyer experience.

Cost of using fulfillment using Amazon (FBA)

While there are advantages to using an FBA, it is important to decide whether this provider's fees decide whether it is appropriate for your business.

Amazon breaks down its storage expenses through measurements (standard and oversized), weight, and time of year. For your items, you can estimate success and storage fees to include these services:

- Taking your order and packing
- Shipping and handling your order
- customer service
- Product returns
- Foot storage per foot per month

For example, a small standard-sized item (such as a pill or book) that is 1 pound or so will have a $ 2.41 fulfillment fee from January-September. A large-scale standard size item ranging from 2GB to 3lb will cost $ 5.26. Standard-size inventory storage fees are $ 0.64 per cubic foot and can increase to $ 2.35 per cubic foot at some point in the holiday months.

However, modifications cost for items offered on any different channel than Amazon.com. The same tablet or book, if sold on your personal website states that you will have to pay an optional fee of $ 7.90 in total to ship in 2 days.

There are different scenarios for applying additional costs. These exceptional cases can cause exchange in popular pricing:

- Oversized gadgets that have special handling fees for shipment.
- There are additional storage fees for stock stored for six months.
- Success and storage prices increase from October to December.

Others may follow fees such as prep service prices or fees for processing customer returns in specific categories.

Clothes items cost an additional $ 0.40 per unit.

Use this chart to see a complete list of FBA costs by product dimension and category. If you will be using FBA for the gadget now offered on Amazon, use this chart for fulfillment costs for multichannel success orders.

Think about your enterprise and the items you sell. If you have very large items, inventory with a long-shelf-life, or a willingness to use FBA, you are going to face additional costs.

Because groups are specialized with many specific types of items, Amazon provides a fulfillment through the Amazon Revenue Calculator that calculates costs and viable revenue from using FBAs. If you already promote on Amazon, this tool is exceptional in that you have some merchandise. It is possible to find a free FBA bulk calculator to test expenses for multiple gadgets at once.

Keep in mind that Amazon revises its expenses almost annually. You like to make positive and you constantly consider costs. The current 2019 fulfillment from the change in Amazon fee is effective from February 15, 2019.

Disadvantages of Using Fulfillment through Amazon

Even though Amazon has one of the best success processes in the world, their FBA provider still has few, unrealistic, threats to sellers on the spot. Make sure you express thoughts on these difficulties before signing up for the service.

Merchandising Merchandise

Whoever buys Amazon's products from their nationwide services can get the item the fastest, which is why they are so efficient. To create some similar efficacy for FBA users, you are given the option of pooling your products.

Commingling combines qualified products from individual marketers for processing and cargo with the help of Amazon. As a seller, it saves the time and effort you put into using FBA authorized labels for each of your gadgets or in any other case to pay Amazon.

Commingling combines qualified products from exceptional agents for processing and cargo through Amazon. As a seller, this saves you time and effort otherwise you spend using the FBA accepted label for each of your items or paying Amazon to do it for you.

Instead of offering labels, you just use an item's barcode, which increases your business with different retailers based on product IDs in swimming pools. Amazon can then store the product strategically and send gadgets of the same product ID to the area that ensures the fastest-shipping time.

For example, a buyer in Ohio selects a product from a seller in Colorado. If Amazon's equipment finds a similar product offered with the help of a seller in Indiana whose product is in a nearby fulfillment center, they will ship the item to the Indiana seller to the buyer. The Colorado seller still receives course sales. Since all gadgets are the same, what is the possible problem?

Product superb control, therefore, becomes very difficult for sellers. The scenarios stated where marketers are forced to close shops, receive poor reviews, or even face hooliganism when counterfeit or broken items are received by customers in exchange for an actual item Is done, which frustrates the seller Amazon.

Be aware: By default, your vendor account is set to use the producer barcode to sing your list. So, your items will be paired with similar merchandise items from other retailers that use manufacturer barcodes. If you are not in favor of implementing your products, you should manually alternate your Amazon barcode option.

Sales Tax Compliance

Another voiced problem of the FBA is income tax compliance. Amazon does not notify agents that many of their warehouses preserve their items. They additionally no longer supply a list of warehouses where goods are intended to be located.

Sellers are then unspecified where they should register for income tax compliance. They do not know at which place the gadgets are saved or where the customers are located after the transaction is completed. This probably exposes retailers to legal responsibility issues.

Long Term Storage Charges and Inventory

As the FBA grows, the area within the success centers becomes more valuable. It is not surprising that Amazon charges you more if your stock sits on their shelves for more than 6 months.

If your items have long-lived lives or if you usually have stale inventory, then you are paying hefty money on rent just to keep the items, especially if it is not going to sell. It is challenging to monitor when this inventory becomes too much of a burden on your backside line. If you have thousands of items, it is difficult to ensure how many tons of inventory you have and you need to reduce the low back.

Preparing Items for Shipment

While Amazon takes care of the whole success method for you, they only do it as soon as they have inventory in their hands. Sellers may battle with preparing and shipping their items to Amazon's fulfillment centers.

You should forecast the items that you think you are going to sell and then the top label and ship them on Amazon. It takes more time, planning and prices to ship your goods to the appropriate warehouses. This is even more difficult if you are sending a stack of products.

Fulfillment Options via Amazon

If you do not offer the use of FBAs, then the pick is really worth taking the time to compare. You can use another third-party success carrier such as Shipwire which provides services similar to FBA. For an in-depth evaluation of FBA options, check out our Book3D Party Fulfillment Services: Fulfillment with the help of Amazon (FBA) Options.

You can also think of solutions that automate every part of your success process. By integrating 3PL vendors like your eCommerce, Marketplace, ERP, and FBA, you can automate approaches such as order management, dropshipping and return management.

Is the FBA Worth your Business?

Just because fulfillment is used through Amazon through a lot of third-party vendors, it does not mean that it is right for your business.

You have to consider its major benefits such as 2-day delivery and its service fees vs. easy returns. Sellers should additionally factor in some of the mentioned troubles with sales tax compliance.

For some, it will probably be a hard priority to use FBA or not. If you determine that FBA is right for you, learn more about how to combine FBA extra tightly with various retail structures such as your ERP, POS and Net Store.

Chapter 3: Determine your Product Range

Selling on Amazon can be a very meaningful channel for brands. So far, many Amazon retailers have played entertainment to win the purchasing arena or charge a large amount of income on a new personal label product, greatly reducing the charge so that no margin exists immediately after the sale.

Amazon made changes to expenses for FBA to sell on Amazon, and to get started.

This information will tell you exactly what Amazon's costs are, how much you will be charged, and how to complete the ideal math to keep your Amazon revenue positive.

Commercial retailers pay variable closing expenses and referral fee percentages ranging from 6% to 25% (average of 13%). Professional vendors additionally pay $ 39.99 per month, although they are exempted from the $ 0.99 per item fee.

1. *Monthly membership fee.*

If you are a professional vendor (someone is planning to promote more than forty gadgets per month), the service provider fee is $ 39.99 per month.

2. *Fee per item.*

Non-professional marketers (i.e. individual sellers) pay $ 0.99 per product sold.

Professional vendors pay $ 0.

3. *Referral fees.*

Amazon referral prices are based on the product category.

Items in unencumbered classes have a per-item minimum referral charge (i.e., marketers pay an increase of the referral price or a minimum per-item referral fee).

Amazon will have either of these two for each item:

Referral fee as a percentage of the selling price: It ranges from 6% to 20% (45% for Amazon devices), but is typically 15%.

Minimum referral fees of both $ 0 or $ 1: Jewelry and watches are the only two categories with a fee of $ 2.

4. Variable Closing Fee.

These strictly follow books, music, videos, DVDs, video games, consoles and software (BMVD products), and will be in accordance with the category, transportation, leisure, location, and type of shipping service used.

5. Supply Fee.

These prices are mainly based on product dimensions and weight.

This fee is usually between $ 2.41 and $ 10 for most products, although the price is going up in 2019.

Why Amazon Sellers Need This Multidimensional Function

However, beyond fees, the biggest reason a lot of organizations lose on Amazon is due to the fact that they use a one-dimensional matrix to determine profitability.

What is the multidimensional method?

The multidisciplinary methodology will help you determine your profitability on SKU degree so that you can make the most knowledgeable venture, including:

- Pricing.
- Inventory management and restocking.
- Management returns.
- Seller talks

Know your cost

If someone asks you if you know your specific cost at the SKU level, will you be able to say yes?

Even the most equipped marketers are missing the hidden values affecting their previous line.

Let's start with a review of the minimum list of fees that should be considered in your monetary model:

1. Direct cost.

Your acquisition price per SKU with shipping.

2. Indirect (overhead) cost.

Warehouse costs, utilities, insurance, bookkeeping, payroll and profit, enterprise travel, corporate commercial enterprise taxes, product sampling, internet development, and more.

3. Amazon fees.

Sales commission, FBA charges, FBA inbound shipping charges, re-product charges, storage fees, return transportation fees (both from the buyer to Amazon Achievement Centers, and from your fulfillment facilities), and settlement costs.

4. The cost of receiving them after receipt of returns.
What do you write or stop writing by not being in a position to promote these back products as new-condition products?

Determining Your Overhead Allocation Cost Per Unit

To calculate this, add your indirect expenses in the last 12 months, and divide that sum by the number of units purchased in the last 12 months.

Use this limit as a rule of thumb - it has to be stabilized on a month-to-month basis.

For example, suppose you have sold 2 billion overhead allocation costs per unit. This is how much cash you already have on the sale of an item you bought or offered.

Typically, we see an overhead allocation fee of between $ 1 - $ 3 per unit.

If your overhead allocation value is more than this, it may decide to evaluate your male or female commercial enterprise costs and how to settle your costs.

For example, let's say that Kathy's Cat Toys is spending thousands of rupees on Amazon-sponsored products each month to force visitors to their Cozy Cat Castle.

However, his return on his investment is three income per month.

Unlike his individual SKUs based on the excessive overhead allocation price for that particular unit, he must decide whether the SKU is actually determined to sell.

Take a Look at your Amazon Fee

All Amazon charges can be drawn from the Vendor Center (Vendor Central> Reports> Payments> View all details) in a time frame of one to two weeks.

Keep in mind that your FBA will cost more for heavier or larger items.

Be sure to reveal any slow-moving SKU, as stale stock may prompt you to charge extra.

Lastly, while some of your values may be SKU-specific, some may not.

Once the prices are calculated through the individual SKU, the discontinued fees should be allocated to all sold equipment.

This is a very easy strategy for profitability calculation and will give you the minimum amount you want to display your fees day to day, or month to month.

In short, evaluate your costs:

- Wholesale cost.
- Inbound / Outbound Shipping.

- Amazon Commission.
- FBA fees.
- Overhead Value Allocation.
- Return-related costs.

Unfortunately, if you do not have a regular pulse on your profitability with the help of SKUs, it can be difficult to quickly modify supplier negotiations, stock management, or product sourcing.

By shifting towards an effigy of profitability with the help of SKU (updated every 3-6 months), there is a good appreciation of the overhead allocation value that you need to use all modern sales, and understanding the impact of the product At your SKU-level and simple profitability, you can emerge as an outstanding vendor.

This understanding will help inform future decisions and teach future shopping.

If Kathy's Cat Toys is promoting a light-weight feather toy that is increasing the minimum FBA fee, has a low overhead fee and sells like a hot cake, Kathy knows to recreate that toy.

However, Cozy Cat Castle which is a heavy, heavy and slow-moving SKU that Kathy no longer shows Consideration when she purchases or even withdraws from the FBA so as not to charge extra.

A lot of small manufacturers tune all these calculations through spreadsheets, although this can be exceptionally inefficient and time-consuming.

Most successful mid-market marketers hire third-party software to help automate this system and determine their true profitability.

Identify Trends that Are Costing You Money

1. Returns.

While some products may also have exorbitant return rates (for example, 20% of orders are returned), you may be in a position to resell all of these items as 'new' status easily if the customer does not open or tamper with the product before returning it.

Other merchandise may also have a lower return rate, but if again (e.g., software, vitamins, underwear) is a complete write-off.

If you are pressurized to resume SKU, because 'after withdrawal' is used, then the value you write will be in the position of not being in a position to generate the proceeds. There is a shortage.

As the goods are returned, you must now return not only the ratio of each SKU but also the value of the per-return or write-off.

This can be determined in vendor central reports or can be computerized through third-party software.

It is mandatory to display the return rates and returns related expenses as these charges at one time will be high enough to warrant the withdrawal of goods from your catalog.

Alternatively, you may also have the option of choosing the section of the fee with which you share return-related price data at your distributor/supplier.

For example, consider that Molly's marionettes have seen an enormous number of returns.

After Molly returns the return analysis, she realizes that she is leaving the money.

Once she removes the troublesome product from her catalog, she gets a 10% increase in profit the following month.

2. Stockout.

Let's look at the examples of how much effect stockouts had on Steve's sporting goods.

Steve is an equestrian Amazon seller with over 5,000 products, and his top seller is a pair of high-end football cleats. The class is flying off the shelves and selling an average of 60 gadgets per month with an income of $ 50 per unit.

On average, Steve remains out of stock for an average of 2.5 days per month on these cleats, equivalent to a $ 1,500 loss in earnings in the direction of the year (12 days = $ 1,500 for x 2.5 months x (50 days x $ 50 / unit)).

If Steve was able to reduce his average stockout time in half per month, he would make an additional $ 50,000 profit every year.

Since "Kate Middleton Effect" is hard to predict, the great solution is to build a buffer in your shopping for strategy and buy more inventory to put together for scenarios like these. Keep in mind that this approach also has drawbacks. If your product does not sell, you threaten to pay those pesky FBA storage fees.

Every retailer knows that when spring starts, winter boot income slows down compared to jaggery in January and rain boots and slippers start flying off the shelves.

For many sellers, this regularly impacts stockouts.

How to stop this stockout scenario:

If you are promoting seasonal items, you would prefer to monitor the modifications in your historical income rank and stay on top of other factors such as weather patterns to predict inventory levels. This allows tracking thread spreadsheets or third-party software.

Sometimes, you will run into dealer problems that are beyond your control.

For example, Nike decided to discontinue your best-selling running shoe or your wholesaler ran out of stock.

How to stop this stockout scenario:

Be the right consumer of your supplier and keep an open trail of communication with them at all times.

In this way, you can be robust to any modifications in their product line or SKU range and adapt your approach accordingly. Most importantly, you will understand that if any of your best-selling items are going to close, it gives you the ability to buy a bunch of additional inventories, so that you can experience this income for as long as possible.

There are two attainable reasons:
Suddenly, Kelly runs out of inventory and you are the top seller on the list. This causes demand to pass through the roof of your blender and you are no longer in a position to hold it, allowing you to go out of stock as well.

The opposite scenario occurs when Amazon sees the success happening with your KitchenAid blender and starts selling similar SKUs. You are no longer able to win a buy box, no counting number of how low you are with your price.

How to fix this stockout scenario:
It is generally necessary to monitor the volumes in sales volume, fee revisions and sales velocity for your SKU.

This will help you catch the first state of affairs as quickly as possible so that you can optimize your strategy.

Depending on your competition, you may wish to raise your price to get more than a profit margin from this momentary spike in sales.

Contestants jumping into a list are becoming more of a common occurrence.

To put this top-notch status together, be constantly on the lookout for opportunities to diversify and expand your portfolio so that skipping a few SKUs won't make or break your business.

The additional risk you incur at the brand, dealer, and SKU levels reduces your risk.

Always scout to promote new manufacturers so that if your satisfactory supplier starts promoting Amazon immediately or if your supplier bites you completely, you have more profitable inventory to depend on in your portfolio.

Know your Metrics

Key Performance Indicators (KPIs) are fundamental to the success of any business.

These metrics can help you consider your success in achieving important goals, allowing you to look at trends or problem areas and test your universal performance.

They are used in all industries, although are particularly beneficial for retail businesses.

The most for-profit Amazon retailers know how to phase their appraisals by brands, suppliers, and buyers, and an evaluation matrix for each of these areas at least once a week.

The most important KPIs to evaluate the fitness of your Amazon business is:

1. List of sales ratios.

This key metric covers many areas of your business.

It shows the overall fitness of your stock and highlights your selling rate.

2. Inventory Turn.

A lower turnover value means worse income and, therefore, more inventory.

3. Gross Margin Return on Investment (GMROI).

GMROI is the ratio used to evaluate inventory profitability.

A multiple ratio means that you are promoting the goods for more than the total fee charged to acquire it.

4. Cash to Cash Cycle.

The Cash to Cash cycle measures the amount of capital invested to move from money to the manufacturing and sales process and then convert into money once more is sold.

This metric appears on the amount of time it takes to boost inventory, the amount of time needed to collect dues, and the size of the organization spent to pay its payments.

The longer your money is for the cash cycle, the longer your money floats.

This ability is leaving you with potentially additional worthwhile investment.

5. Days of Inventory (DOI).

Quantity on hand / (Sales during period/period)

This KPI will help you to see an item in common days before selling it in stock.

This is extremely useful in setting order limits to ensure that you are not overstocking or stocking out of your inventory.

Inventory (DOI) days are too high for companies not tracking KPIs.

Profitability Leaks

Tracking your metrics is important due to the fact that dollars are in the details.

While these important points may also take minutes, when mistakes are added, they can create or destroy your business.

Here are a few times neglected profitability leaks for Amazon sellers:

Lost or Damaged Gadgets returned: Occasionally, objects returned by customers are either incorrectly broken or transferred, and sellers of those gadgets never receive them.

You do not acquire your refund: When a customer returns one of your products to Amazon, Amazon immediately returns it to the buyer who paid the amount paid for the item. However, at any point in time that any refunded is returned to the seller's account.

Amazon no longer receives your shipment in full: it is common for components of your cargo to be lost or broken through

Amazon's achievement centers. Verifying the SKU, you send to the FBA suite with Amazon shipped is fundamental.

1. Vendor negotiation.

Put all data on the table and conduct an audit on all your suppliers.

This will help you to place in areas where you can negotiate to get higher deals.

For example, in the example below the seller needs to be in a position to leverage his large income volume and a five-year relationship to negotiate higher payment terms.

2. Product Sourcing.

Now that you know that the metrics we've used as your most profitable SKU, inform your future purchases for decisions using your findings.

lower your product mark or your manufacturers go out of business, you will see a huge drop in income.

3. Historical profitability trends.

If you feel that your purple oven income is decreasing over time, then it is time to consider whether you prefer to recreate that product.

Remember that all merchandise has a survival cycle - the key is to pay interest for trends

4. Consider a third-party solution.

Reviewing Vendor Central is often not completely adequate and spreadsheets can be a pain to change and manage.

Save time with the help of automated methods that can be more effectively managed through technology.

Chapter 4: Calculate Amazon Revenue

As an Amazon seller, the biggest choice you have to make is whether to fulfill the orders yourself or via the FBA. Each option comes with pros and cons, although ultimately the decision is based solely on profits. two

In fact, some goods that are pleasant through the FBA should end up with a very little result, no longer to indicate that in some cases it should also result in losses.

On the other hand, the FBA comes with such a blessing that it is not possible to simply bypass it. So, how can you decide?

Fortunately, Amazon practices a very clear FBA fee policy. In addition, you can use the Amazon FBA calculator to check product profitability, margins, and estimated satisfaction expenses when delivering your orders through both FBA or FBM.

Selling on Amazon FBA Fees

Before knowing how to calculate fees, you should understand why FBA is better than self-fulfillment and what charges apply in the market.

The FBA stands for Fulfillment through Amazon and refers to an application where the marketplace manages your orders and fulfills them on your behalf. This brings some benefits for you and your buyers.

Some of the key benefits include:

No worries about inventory storage; Amazon's warehouse featuring your products will have areas around them.

No worries about the packing and delivery of your products, as Amazon will do all that for you.

There is no concern about customer-provider or returns. Amazon provides a patron provider for all FBA orders and manages returns on your behalf.

Eligibility to join Amazon Prime. Since Amazon has entered your products fast, your business is a hero, so you can grow your patron pool.

Win purchase box. As a key member, you are more likely to win the Buy Box.

Better customer engagement. By selling their merchandise the FBA builds more trust towards customers, which sooner or later results in more sales.

How does FBA work?

To be part of the Amazon FBA, you must select from your Amazon seller central account in the software. Then, you have to pack, label, and ship your goods to Amazon's warehouse.

All this is done through vendor central. Here, you will have the opportunity to track your inventory, set alerts and replenish your stock as necessary every time.

If you do not like to label your products, Amazon can do so on your behalf for an additional fee.

Now, the fine step is that once Amazon receives your items, they are immediately available for sale. From now on, you have no different concerns than placing orders and increasing your profit. Although it is convenient to think, it all comes at a cost.

Amazon for fee

Amazon calculates its FBA costs based on the weight and measurement of each unit you sell. They are damaged in two types of fees, success charges, and month-to-month stock charges.

Supply fee

Does Amazon have costs to deal with your order, such as picking and packing units, handling fees for transportation and any product returns, dealing with consumer service and management?

Clothing items, as well as gadgets with lithium batteries, are included at additional prices of $ 0.40 and $ 0.11 per unit, respectively.

Monthly inventory fee

The 2D section of the FBA charges you for a monthly stock storage fee. These are calculated from cubic feet, so the smaller your equipment is and the less you sell, the less you have to pay.

When Amazon calculates your inventory storage charge, those elements come to mind, in fact, the size of your unit, the average volume of each day, as well as the season.

All of the above fees refer to general FBA fulfillment, but you also have different options. In addition to the comprehensive program, Amazon also offers:

Multi-channel fulfillment

Allows you to sell products on your e-commerce and fulfill them through Amazon.

FBA Small & Light is a program designed for retailers that promote small, light-weight and affordable products with a few points of $ 15 or less. These FBA fees come as an option for dealers who might not otherwise have followed the FBA.

FBA Subscribe and Save: is a software designed to help agents decorate customer retention. You can sign up to offer discounts on eligible FBA products to repeat customers.

Each of the three choice programs described above comes with a specific fulfillment cost and can also open doors to new opportunities.

In addition to the FBA, you may additionally decide to fulfill your own orders. You do not have to pay any costs for Amazon; however, this solution should be more expensive to you except that you promote very small items that you can keep in your home.

You can use one of the many Amazon FBA calculators to decide which fulfillment option is the most profitable.

9 Free Amazon FBA Calculator You Should Try

A faster way to keep your Amazon costs can be to manage and decide which breakthrough technology can work at first-rate with the help of Amazon FBA calculator. Here 9 you can use for free.

1. Amazon revenue calculator

Fulfillment by Amazon Revenue Calculator is a web app distributed with the help of Amazon's Vendor Central. It is very easy to use and gives you a clear idea of what you will spend FBA. The calculator indicates in detail whether you should opt for FBA or FBM. In addition to a clear comparison between options, you can additionally use this calculator to decide what your product will be worth.

Features:

- Simple and intuitive interface
- It lets you search for a product and calculate success fees and profits based on ASIN or keywords.
- Clear chart of revenue, cost, seller's income, and Internet profit
- Available to US, CA and MX dealers

2. Vendor via FBA Calculator Seller

Another reliable calculator is the seller to consider. It comes in both web or chrome extension variants. The pure model lets you search for merchandise based primarily on their ASIN or Amazon links. Click the Calculate FBA Profits button to get a clear idea of fees.

If you want to test FBA fees while shopping for products, deploy the Chrome extension and click on it every time you find an attractive product.

Features:

- Hands-free calculator in both Internet and Chrome extension types
- FBA vs FBM Fee & Fee Overview
- An accurate estimate of your potential income and internet profit
- Product margins and profitability are easy to analyze
- Available to sellers of US, UK, MX, CA, IN, DE, ES, FR, IT and JP

3. *Jungle Scout FBA Profit Calculator*

Unlike other calculators on this list, the one offered through Jungle Scout comes as a downloadable XLS file. You'll grab it in your mailbox and can use it to get an accurate estimate of product profit, internet margin, net profit, and FBA fees.

Features:

- Super-easy to use calculator both online and offline
- A comprehensive breakdown of all appreciable prices and predicted profit or loss
- The downloadable file can be used on laptops, PCs and cellular devices

4. *AMZScout FBA Fee Calculator*

One of Jungle Scout's main competitors, AMZScout has not overlooked the opportunity to create a free FBA fee calculator. And it also outperformed JS. It comes as a Chrome extension and is equivalent to the one offered with the help of SellerApp.

Features:

- A one-click estimate of your income and income level
- Full figures on Amazon's commission
- Calculation of fees based on product dimensions and weight
- It returns all calculations at once in the expansion window
- This calculator uses data received from vendor central immediately.

5. *Viral Launch Amazon FBA Calculator*

Viral Launch is one of the most well-known companies of equipment and services for Amazon sellers. Most of it comes from an excise tax, but what you can get for free is the Amazon FBA calculator. All you have to do is, if you wish, enter an ASIN or product link to accurately estimate your margins and profits, the cost of the landed unit and click the button.

Features:

- This calculator indicates realistic estimates of all the costs you want to expect.

- Ideal to use to get an idea of the FBA costs and upfront funds needed by new vendors
- Viral launch market intelligence and product research tool

6. *SaleCalc*

This calculator does not let you calculate your estimated profit for a specific product, but for any product in a category. This is no longer true like other calculators on this list, but we have preserved it because it is very intuitive and easy to use.

Features:

- Results displayed in both listing and design modes
- It suggests cost, income, and profit based on product category, weight, and price.
- You can calculate your margin mainly based on delivery credit or FBA

7. **ShipBob Amazon FBA Cost Calculator**

Amazon is coming up as an alternative to the seller central calculator, via ShipBob as it bases it effects on fees for FBA services that Amazon practiced in previous months. To supply accurate results, it performs calculations based on the different types of orders you receive, the dimensions of the package, average item weight, and other variables that may also impact FBA charges.

Features:

- Comprehensive results displayed in the monthly breakdown sheet
- It calculates your monthly income and margin
- It estimates your revenue and profit growth

8. Fetcher Mileage Calculator

While the Fetcher Profit Calculator does an exceptional job in calculating your manageable Amazon FBA, this device is designed to calculate your profit. In doing so, it takes into account many variables that other calculators do not even consider, such as your upfront costs, constant costs, variable prices with FBA fees, and advertising and marketing costs, so that you can actually make an informed selection. Can. About product profitability.

Features:

- Accurate estimation of product profitability based on several variables
- Free to use with an email subscription
- Completing other Fetcher tools for more complete appreciation of the gain or loss receivable

9. *Salary Dynamics Amazon Profit Calculator*

Just fill in the required details, and you'll get a full stop of all the costs and benefits you can expect.

Features:

- Simple and convenient for Amazon UK sellers to use a dedicated interface
- Salary Dynamics additionally proposes a simple Amazon FBA calculator that will only inform you how much you can fully rely on to pay for Amazon fulfillment.
- The final benefit calculation includes postage and VAT charges, with different charges viewed through different calculators.

Amazon FBA calculators may also not necessarily be accurate, but they are clearly a useful tool to use when identifying the profitability of a product. A simple way to obtain more accurate estimates is to use multiple calculators and evaluate the results. Whether you just determine to use one or a few, it is positive that they can help you optimize your business.

A Step-by-Step Amazon FBA Calculator for Sellers

As an enterprise owner, you have a laundry listing filled with overhead expenses to hold running:

- Operating cost
- Utilities
- Payroll + benefits
- Insurance
- journey
- Taxes
- Marketing
- Web development
- Storage
- The rent

Now, it's time to get into the funny gritty of FBA vs Non-FBA and determine that ASINS needs to be FBA, and that doesn't deserve it.

Step 1. Calculate your total cost per product

You will need to calculate your average charge per product to decide whether the FBA is really worth it to ship. Add all of the following.

- acquisition cost
- Cost to buy inventory
- The cost of getting it for your convenience
- Cost of the ship to an amazon delivery center
- Shipping & Delivery
- The packaging
- Markdowns

Once you understand these costs, you can start drilling to decide how much you are earning per product or SKU.

Step 2. Divide the total cost of your product by the number

Once you calculate all your character product costs, divide that variation by the full range of gadgets purchased in the final year. The end result is how a good deal is counted on each product to price you in resources.

Plug data into Amazon Seller Fee Calculator in

Step 3. Seller Central

Head to Cellar Central and use the specialty of reviews to pull your entire fee for the product for a period of one week.

Are you paying more than 30% at the expense of a product?

When a per product is added to your allocated fee, are you in a position to make money on that SKU?

It all depends on your goals and can be very product-specific. A $ 10 object that is huge and heavy will symbolize a large percentage of your margin, while a small and light item sold for $ 30 will symbolize a very small percentage spent.

For this reason, excessive ASP (average selling price) is a major consideration for FBA inventory selection. Popular gadgets that promote quickly are awesome for the FBA. It no longer experiences sending something to Amazon that is probably not meant to be promoted and may also reduce storage by reducing storage fees.

While some dealers dispute this, claiming that gadgets with lower sales rank are the best to sell by the FBA, on the basis that their promotional prospects are usually significantly increased due to their Amazon Prime "teaser.

Chapter 5: Find a Supplier

Understand the Distribution Channels of Your Industry

There are many approaches that can go from a product manufacturer to a retailer. Not all wholesalers serve the same market. Understanding your industry's distribution channels, and understanding where you fit into the presented chain can help you locate the appropriate wholesaler for your retail or online business.

Different types of wholesalers include:

Manufacturer: For some products, you can buy at once from the manufacturer. It is basically a "boutique" that does - buy from small (sometimes one person) manufacturers.

Importer / Exclusive Distributor: In some industries, an agency may have sole rights to import and distribute the product in a positive country. Some retailers can promote without delay, although more often, they establish or sell to small neighborhood wholesalers.

Wholesalers / regional distributors: There are usually regional wholesalers who take delivery of boxcar-sized lots, break them up and promote truckload containers of products to nearby wholesalers.

Jobbers, "wagon peddlers": These people deliver every day to local grocers and retail brick-and-mortar stores.

Each product industry has its own special distribution channel. Some shops will go in sufficient quantities to pass on to jobbers, or perhaps in a small industry, importers promote directly to retailers.

When you first start, you can shop at smaller prices from smaller wholesalers. As your range increases, you will be in a position to offer better pricing and/or a ladder to a larger wholesaler.

Try Producer First

You will probably start at the source as well. If you are promoting branded items, go directly to the manufacturer of the product. They will likely promote you, relying on your minimum order requirements.

If you are too young for them or they only promote mounted distribution channels, ask for a list of distributors you can contact. By starting at Supply (Manufacturer), you can either get the lowest expense or at least get the list of the most reliable distributors to close your search.

The fewer humans you have to go through, the lower your price, which can make you more aggressive in the market.

You can also consider selecting a smartphone to make an initial outreach call, or to follow up with humans that you've deleted along with your initial emails. It cannot harm them to tell you that you are doing research and also finding different competitors; This can help you get better value, even if you are starting small.

Try to Search for Wholesalers on Google

As mentioned above, you can start your initial search with some common Google search terms. As you delve deeper into your research, you can potentially become more specific about the products you want.

Conduct Google for "wholesale" or "distributor" phrases, as well as some key phrases from your products or niche. Try product name, mannequin number, and company name. Go through each result and look at the "bulk account" hyperlink or the quantity of an electronic mail tackle or smartphone, where you can find more information. In the unusual case of the fact that the facts are difficult to find or no longer readily available, you should do a WHOIS search to find the website's contact information. Then, additional viable wholesalers that you locate better will be able to save you and get an experience of what the general industry expenses are, as well as get competitive quotes.

Look for Wholesale Lots on eBay

If all else fails, some shops or small wholesalers will sell your product on eBay.

Since eBay often targets retail consumers, the wholesale options you will explore here are generally suitable for very small retailers. But if you're just getting started, eBay can find it easy to dip your toes into your e-commerce and start shipping products It is easy to make contact with them on eBay to find out if this is indeed the case.

Check out The Major B2B Marketplace

start over; It is an 800-pound gorilla B2B marketplace of manufacturers, importers and wholesale distributors. Other B2B markets include Global Source (USA), Buyer Zone (USA), EC21 (Korea), EC Plaza (Korea) and Busy Trade (Hong Kong).

When thinking about wholesale distributors always appear on some sources.

Join Industry Groups, Forums, and Other Business Networks

Other retailers are not keen on sharing dealer data with competitors, so you will be one of those insiders. Take part in the on-line forums, they can be a great source of free records and help various humans along the ride in this market. You can also create your LinkedIn profile and start making connections, subscribe to enterprise newsletters, and usually build your professional network.

Subscribe to Trade Publications of Your Industry

Get every magazine or newspaper that targets retailers in your industry. Each advertiser in the magazine will be a product manufacturer or distributor who wants to reach you. You should have a few dozen choices of advertisements behind the magazine Remember, everything you need from your first supplier is a product that you can put to profit. This may not be the best wholesale price for you, but it doesn't matter initially.

Whether it is manufacturing their product or searching for suppliers to buy wholesale, they are not always easy to find.

Includes Manufacturers, Wholesalers, And Distributors

There are a ton of useful resources online that you can find on Google. But before starting, there are some things you should know and decide.

First of all, you should determine what type of supplier you are looking for.

There are several options, the most common are:

-A *producer* to produce his product idea;

-A *supplier* (who can also be a manufacturer), *wholesaler* or *distributor* to buy already existing brands and products;

-A *drop shipper* to supply products and fulfill orders for pre-existing brands and products.

Domestic vs Foreign Suppliers

When you seek suppliers if you plan to manufacture or wholesale, you will need to decide whether you want to source from domestic or foreign. Expatriates can refer to any place abroad.

Typically, and for the purpose of this designation, foreign suppliers are located in Asian countries such as China, India, and Taiwan. Because it is often cheaper to source your products abroad, especially in these countries. But there is a lot more to the decision than investment per unit and cost per unit.

Both domestic and foreign sourcing have their advantages and disadvantages:

Domestic Sourcing

Benefits

- Producing high quality and labor standards.
- Easy communication with the language barrier.
- Marketing appeal in North America
- Easy to verify reputable manufacturers.
- Fast shipping time.
- High Intellectual Property Rights Protection.
- Greater payment protection and support.
  Disadvantages

- High manufacturing costs.
- Fewer product choices (there are many items that are not yet made in North America).
- Overseas sourcing

Online Home Directory

- Thomasnet
- Manufacturer's line
- MFG
- Kompass

Online Foreign Directory

- Oberlo
- Alibaba
- AliExpress
- Indiamart
- Source

Google

Over the years, we have become accustomed to being able to easily search Google and find what we are looking for in the first few search results. However, many suppliers did not keep pace with the Internet or Google's algorithm changes. Their websites are usually outdated, sparse on information and not optimized by the search engines.

So how do you search for suppliers on Google? Probably for the first time, you want to find two web pages in Google search results and beyond. You would additionally be in favor of using multiple search terms. For example, terms like a wholesale, wholesaler, and distributor can also be used interchangeably, so you have to search for them all.

Local Library

You can also think about visiting your local library. Many libraries pay a monthly subscription fee to line trade and manufacturer directories that usually you won't get the right of entry, or you won't have to pay for it.

Call your local library ahead of time and ask if they have received access to this type of personal directories. For larger libraries, you may need to negotiate with the Department of Business Enterprise and Technology.

Referral

Some excellent leads may come from referrals. Don't be afraid to ask for connections in your specialist network if they have a recommendation, or if they understand someone who might be. Look for individuals who have determined success in the area around you and want to see if they are willing to share their contacts.

Social networks have made it very difficult to get the word out so make sure to use these channels. Join Facebook businesses and other online communities of e-Commerce enterprise owners and see if everyone has glowing reviews.

As you start searching for suppliers, even if they are not appropriate in size for you, be positive to ask them if they can lead you in the right direction. He probably has amazing contacts due to his ability in the industry and it would be comfortable to refer you to an option that could be a high fit.

Sometimes manufacturers and suppliers can also list their products through the NAICS code which can make it simpler to build your product and find suppliers, especially if you are using specialist directories; NAICS listings can be viewed in your neighborhood library or online.

Planning your initial investigation can increase your chances of getting a response and correct information.

Here are some essential questions for your email to reflect on consideration:

-What is your minimum order quantity?

Also referred to as a MOQ, you prefer to make positive the minimum order quantity is manageable for you, and that you may have the money for them. This minimum order quantity may depend heavily on the product and supplier, so it is important to ask in advance.

-What is your sample pricing?

You will like samples to see before making a full prospect. The sample price range is dependent on the product and supplier.

-What is your production value?

One of the most essential questions is how much your products will cost.

-What are your charge terms?

Many suppliers will require new organizations to pay for full order upfront. This is important to recognize because the stock is a fundamental value for e-Commerce startups. You additionally want to ask if they can give a price quote on future orders.

Suppliers are bombarded all the time with email quote requests from flamboyant shoppers who are just kicking the tires' so it is no longer uncommon for many suppliers to respond to every request. The lack of supplier feedback from new eCommerce entrepreneurs is a frequent complaint.

So how do you stay away from being ignored? There are some things you need to keep away from getting from suppliers for the first time:

Pay attention to what you care about the most, such as a small print of the source you are trying for.

Asking too much: Requests for supplier production are not consistently smooth. It is important to ask for some expenses for several quantities, however, stay away from asking for too many or too many quotes. Ask honestly what you need to do to fit between you and the supplier.

Asking for very little: If you ask for a quotation properly of the supplier's minimum order, then you are in danger of being met with silence. If you have not decided whether your request is too small, consider giving them a quick call or sending them an email before asking what their minimum order is.

Finally, if you are contacting a provider from abroad, keep in mind that in many cases, they may be in addition to using applications to translate your email as your answer. Keeping your email concise, concise, well-formatted, and error-free will no longer only help the creator, but will ultimately provide you with higher replies and replies.

Also, when asking your questions, categorizing them is high-quality. In this way, they can answer each number without problems, keeping questions and verbal exchange easy and orderly.

Negotiate Minimum Order Quantity

If you are searching for a provider for the first time, you are going to quickly research the minimum order quantity (Moq). It is no longer unique to require dedication to purchase thousands of devices for your first order dependent on the manufacturer and the product and the manufacturer.

Moms challenge this when you are obliged to cash or favor to start a small purchase and check the market before making a big purchase. Properly the factors that MOQ are almost always negotiable.

Before you negotiate, understand why the provider has imposed the minimum. Is it because there is a lot of work? Or perhaps it is because they choose to work with big buyers. Understanding the objectives behind the minimum will help you improve their situation and allow you to negotiate and propose a great counter offer.

Once you are better informed about your supplier's status, you can reduce the order quantity. The agreement may allow the provider to deposit for a larger order, but produce smaller quantities at a time or charge more per unit.

Have you Found Your First Partner?
Sourcing to suppliers and producers is a specialized process, and for many, a new experience. Trying to get between suppliers that are a suitable suit is an essential decision for your new commercial venture and is usually not easy to find.

When you collide with lifeless ends or brick splits in most cases, it is easy to try to shut it down, just so you need a little more endurance and persistence to find the best collaborator for your new business.

Chapter 6: Open an Amazon Seller account & Sign Up for Amazon FBA

Before you leap into headfirst and start selling on Amazon, there are several steps we encourage any potential seller to take before formalizing the seller account registration process.

Required Paperwork (Amazon Seller Account Checklist)

To get through the full registration technique for an Amazon seller account, you'll need a bunch of stats with no hassle available, including:

1. Business Information.
Contact your hooliganism name, handling, and information

2. Email.
An email tackle that can be used for this organization account. This email account needs to be set up in advance, as you'll start receiving Amazon's important emails almost immediately.

3. Credit Card.
Internationally chargeable savings card with a valid billing address. If the credit score card variation is not valid, Amazon will cancel your registration.

4. Phone Number.
A smartphone range where you can be reached during this registration process. Also, turn off your phone for the duration of registration.

5. Tax ID.
Including your tax identification information, your social security number or your company's federal tax ID number. The method of registration will be a short description of the "1099-K

Tax Document Interview", to keep your tax identification information.

I encourage you to communicate with a tax attorney or tax accountant who is on-line seller tax nexus issues (e.g., salestaxandmore.com, catchingclouds.net, peisnerjohnson.com) or one of the tax remittance organizations Is the one that can provide you with the most contemporary Amazon tax nexus records (e.g., taxjar.com, avalara.com, Taxify.co, vertexsmb.com).

1.Where do you layout to send Amazon order returns?
Who in your team will manage Amazon customer inquiries?
The key now is not just to have all the answers, but to also respect Amazon's requirements to respond to all patron inquiries within 24 hours of any day of the year.
Therefore, figuring out which factor (with viable backup) is a mandatory operational problem that must be addressed before opening your Amazon seller account.

2. If you diagram to use Amazon Fulfillment through the Amazon program, will you co-combine your products?
I highly recommend the use of FBA, given its manageable visibility to 100MM + Amazon Prime customers.

Amazon offers FBA dealers this potentially fatal option of sending products to Amazon's fulfillment centers, where they may have co-mingle with other FBA sellers' products.

In addition, counterfeit or low-grade versions of your goods may result in a combination of what you are selling.

Unfortunately, if a co-milling unit is obtained to fulfill an order on your account, you are left to explain to Amazon why a patron complained about receiving a counterfeit item.

You need to work very quickly because of this problem. If you set out to use FBA, but do not use the co-mingled ("sticker-free") option, then you need to use your "stickered" FBA account. Got to sign to come. From developing their first-ever FBA shipment to Amazon before.

While it is possible to create a sticky account later, it can quickly become very difficult if you have already sent some products to FBA as a sticker-free product.

3. Do you layout to use the name DBA (as a business) to operate your Amazon seller account?

While some businesses have official reasons for using an exceptional customer-facing name, Amazon is also a surrounding area where many marketers purposefully hide their identities.

Reasons for doing so are not to try to make the manufacturers know that they are selling online, or that the company is actually a reseller and not favor their individual retail peers to believe that they are directly selling to the consumer online Product is selling.

4. Have you checked to see if the merchandise you sketched to the list is in the classes that Amazon bought?

Amazon has restrictions that can sell in positive categories, and as long as the system is generally commendable, it is important to acknowledge that if your favored categories are gated, inspecting you for being ungated Will happen.

You will not take long to determine whether you have a problem with the exact brand and SKU.

You can trade your catalog or close your account if Amazon is limiting the products you want to sell.

Important Knowledge and Skills for Amazon Sellers

The Amazon marketplace has its own set of guidelines and rules, although there is also this individual combination of capabilities that each and every seller needs to master fast enough to be profitable and long-lasting.

Contains:

1. Stellar advertising content material for building product listings.

If your merchandise is new in the Amazon catalog (it is easy to take a look through searching for your brand or UPC in the Amazon.com search bar), then you might want to come up with content material for areas such as product title, Bullet points, product descriptions and familiar keywords (for optimizing SEO on your listing).

You will also need product pictures for your listing - see the Support Pictures page, including Amazon for reference, but we want marketers to display a picture as well as a lifestyle as well as a product if possible. Encourage.

This lifestyle photo enhances primary photographs that have strict requirements, such as a white background, no branding, and a count of at least 500 × 500 pixels.

2. A clear appreciation of your product sourcing path.

If your merchandise sells properly on Amazon, do you understand how to refill quickly enough to keep it out of considerable stockout periods?

If you specialize in close-out and one-time purchases, you also may not be in a position to easily replenish the equivalent SKU, although there should be well-defined processes to include new inventory, because Your Amazon Cache function improves.

3. An option on the diagram or not to sell more similar items to you.

If yes, then you would be in favor of taking advantage of Amazon's replenishment warning tools inside Seller Central, as well as various external forecasting tools, such as standalone options from www.forecastly.com or any of these multichannel inventory/order management tools Will integrate into

4. An evolving method for locating and addressing stale inventory.

While everyone needs their goods to sell, the fact remains that there will be something consistently that does not promote properly and liquidation or offer on other channels to assist in converting stock capital back into working capital. should be done.

Amazon has the know-how of stale inventory to help FBA marketers, while Non-FBA Amazon sellers want their inventory to be shown to the parent via SKU if it can be promoted for faster sales.

5. Understanding of the basic cost structure, including overhead costs.

A lot of retailers on Amazon only point out the basics of SKU-level profitability, due to a combined view of the seller's universal profitability, as an option from a pinpoint perspective on which percent of SKUs power the profits, while it Understanding which products are really expensive to sell on Amazon

Many Amazon marketers do not stop their profitability until the year their accountant announces the closing number, with luck to the seller's relief.

It is integral for retailers to obtain their overhead costs and bring them together, and understand that these changes need to be integrated into meeting the prices that a seller promotes on Amazon.

6. Know that you are already selling the same SKU on Amazon.

Shockingly often, new agents join Amazon and list their products, only to find that the level or kind of competition on their listings makes it possible for the new seller to make any income or any margin. Is not.

Before opening an Amazon seller account, I strongly encourage each seller to take a look at their intended list on Amazon to see if Amazon Retail is already selling these items.

If so, now walking away from those items is quality.

7. After knowing how much time you need to get on the list after being registered as an Amazon seller.

A new seller does not cost until the end of the first month on Amazon, at some point the seller has made their product available and activated with at least some salable inventory.

If you open your account and do not list your products, you will not be charged for opening your specialist seller's account.

Why is there no graph to make a bunch of investments in the first 30 days to move forward in your account?

Finally, realizing that revenue feedback is important to Amazon in monitoring the performance of all new vendors, I encourage each and every new seller to sign up for a number of inexpensive comment comments that allow each customer Sellers to send requests for feedback.

Contains:

- Feedbackgenius.com
- Feedbackfive.com

- Salesbacker.com
- Bqool.com

All of these can help a seller give customer feedback, and show Amazon that the seller is performing properly against Amazon's performance standards, along with keeping customers happy.

From here, you will love digging into unique Amazon methods:

- Buy Winning Box
- Determining your income outlook (e.g. retail intermediation).
- Choosing the right products.

Common Amazon Seller Frequently Asked Questions

What is amazon seller central?

Amazon Seller Central is where character sellers, brands, and retailer's login to Amazon.com to manipulate and list their products.

What is the Amazon seller return policy?

Amazon requires third-party vendors to offer the following withdrawal technologies:

- Return inside the United States.
- Prepaid Return Label.
- Provide a full refund for inquiries to return the item.

With the help of the Amazon (FBA) business model, fulfillment continues to grow in popularity and for the exact reason. Basically, it is equivalent to a simple e-commerce business. But, alternatively to fulfill orders with the help of one, Amazon stores your products for you and even selects, packs, and ships them to customers.

This makes it very easy for you to build your business without having to worry about the logistics of warehouses, packaging materials, couriers, etc. With non-public labeling, you have the chance to create your very own company and website, which increases your business fees.

What is Fulfillment through Amazon?

The FBA Enterprise model lets you leverage Amazon's strong distribution community and consumer base. As stated, Amazon will store your products, fulfill orders and even supply to a patron provider, so you have to join hands with every factor of the business.

What is this skill for entrepreneurs is that you can obviously work like a giant enterprise without the headache of being one? You can be the focal point in exploring product opportunities while Amazon handles the rest on your behalf.

In a typical e-commerce business, you have to determine the logistics of sending products to your customers in a timely manner. However, with FBA, Principal members are dispatched to their door within two to five days.

Another frequent task with an e-Commerce shop is that listing and recording additional products for sale can increase the complexity of your business. With FBA, you only have to ship the products to Amazon's warehouse, and the organization will take over from there. You can expand your product scheduling without any difficulty, including your workload.

Create an Amazon Seller Account

First things first: To grow and run your FBA business, you will need to create an Amazon seller account. Go to Amazon's website, scroll down to the footer and the title seems to be "Make Money with Us." Next, click on the hyperlink that reads "Sell on Amazon".

At this point, you can sign up as either "Personal" or "Professional". When you indicate "Personal", you will no longer be charged a monthly membership fee. If you are searching to build an enterprise. After a long haul, you will love signing up as a "professional". The first month is free, and after that, it is $ 39.99 per month as well to boost fees.

Also, the method of signup is very straightforward. Follow the on-screen guidelines and the entire setup.

Uncover Product Possibilities and Set Your Own Private Label

There are many unique ways to leverage the FBA model, but the most popular method is individual labeling. The thinking is to establish a brand or label, practice it on your product and promote it on Amazon.

First of all, you will need to do your Amazon product research. This is the most necessary step for various reasons. If you enter an unpopular product category and sell a product for more than your competition, you can lose cash for that product. If you take the time to find a popular product category, do a competitive analysis, learn about product evaluation and get information about a product that you can improve or promote at a better price than you have Candy location is determined.

Another well-known way to promote products through Amazon is with retail intermediation - purchasing a brand recognition product and flip to Amazon for profit. This is a very easy way to make cash on Amazon, at least in the short term.

With personal labeling, you want capital. Ordering private label products can be worth thousands of dollars to you, but if you're looking to build a property that can be sold later, this is the course you're in favor of going into.

If you do not keep the goods in stock, you cannot make cash, so you want to make sure that the long time between the placement and transport of the order is as short as it can be.

Tips to Grow and Grow Your FBA Business

-Pursue your passion; if you enjoy doing it, you will live with it for a long time. Find a product category that hobbies and makes you excited.

-Increase your product offerings; you will want to do the right research for each new product you offer. The danger of your business being overstocked may be established in just one product.

-Improve your best sellers rank; BSR is an important metric for both your customers and sales. This is also an important aspect when it comes time to promote your business. Buyers will see a steady increase in your BSR rank over time.

-Create your own manufacturer website; when you move to make your private label product offering larger, you will choose to create a professional, dedicated website for your business. This gives you another way of marketing your products, and can additionally make your business attractive to practical buyers.

-Become an Amazon Associate; Increase your revenue by converting to affiliate with Amazon. See customers for your goods from your site, and start earning.

Earning Potential

How much do FBA business owners earn? What is the income potential of an FBA business?

Spencer Hubbs of Nikke Pursuits reviews that he was able to make about $ 40,000 within 30 days of the start of his FBA business. Chris Guthrie from UpFuel earned around $ 3,000 within 30 days. Feedback founder James Amazio dropped from zero to $ 50,000 a month in just eight months.

These results are not always specific, although they demonstrate that it is feasible to build a five-, six- or even seven-figure commercial enterprise using the FBA model.

Chapter 7: Create and Optimize Your Amazon Listings

Want your product to rank high in Amazon search results? You can improve rankings (Amazon SEO, or search engine optimization) as well as increase traffic and sales by carefully optimizing your product listings.

Information: Provide all the necessary information for the purchase decision

Communication (Benefits / Benefits): Highlight the article's benefits and USP in detail. How do your product features help potential buyers? How do they really benefit from them?

Presentation: current and structured information so customers can get it quick and easy

Additional content options are available to vendors for high-quality product descriptions. *Results*: Much better options for showing products and brands, and for using cross-selling.

When optimizing product content, it is necessary to keep in mind how it will appear on mobile devices. Texts (such as bullet points and product descriptions) are short enough so that the most important information is always listed first.

Main image: relevant to CTR and CR. The main image can only represent the original product and must comply exactly with Amazon's minimum requirements.

Some important examples are various angles, uses and benefits, environment, lifestyle, and social interaction, proportions, special features, and benefits, embedding details and packaging.

You can use parcel inserts to prompt customers for reviews or advertising on product testing platforms.

Always make sure you stay within Amazon's review guidelines, especially with the latter method. Amazon also offers its own fee-based program for sellers and sellers to generate reviews:

In particular, you should comment on negative customer reviews. As a trader or manufacturer, you can combine your own point of view and shed a better light on the review. It also shows good customer service and can persuade the customer to revise the review or remove it altogether; vendors must regularly address unanswered questions to get customers the right answer.

Chapter 8: Create an FBA Shipping Plan

They frequently revise their fees, conduct research, and efficiently scout for one-of-a-kind products, carefully aligning with their promotional objectives while enhancing their marketing approach, and large profits. One way to earn is to automate the enterprise method.

Amazon's E-Commerce Prominence Keeps Growing

According to the latest reviews published through Statista, Amazon posted full net sales of US $ 56.6 billion in its previous quarter, up from the US $ 51.04 billion in the prior quarter.

Last year, Amazon.com alone generated the US $ 178 billion in total revenue, making it the largest e-retailer in the US (Source: Feedweiser)

With this data, it is clear that Amazon will push its development forward, creating high prospects for third-party dealers on the e-commerce pulse. So, vendors extra, higher competition.

Therefore, as a seller, it is necessary to understand how to create and optimize product listings that can drive additional traffic and convert better. In addition, it is also extra vigilant as a seller of what other sellers have to do on the Amazon marketplace.

Doing so will help dealers gain additional visibility, experience room for improvement and development, and unveil the tricks, drills, and tools that other agents are using to better operate.

Introducing Amazon's A9 Algorithm

According to Amazon's subsidiary A9.com - "Our work starts long before a consumer performs a query. We are analyzing the data, looking at the patterns of previous site visitors, and even prior to indexing the textual content describing each product prior to each product on our list, the buyer also decided to search is

Like search engine algorithms, even Amazon has a set of guidelines to rank its products based on users' queries.

One of the concepts of A9 is relevance and Amazon strives to achieve high-quality effects for its users.

Their rating algorithm is designed to combine robotically with exceptional relevance features. The structured facts in their lists present them with the basic elements needed to produce great results for their users.

The algorithm additionally learns from its prior search patterns and asks its customers to show significant results.

Factors for A9 Algorithm

Although Amazon may not uncover its entire recipe about the A9, there are some factors that play an important function in determining your conversion and sales success. These elements are:

1. Text match relevance

"Relevance" plays an essential role, as stated above. To check how appropriate the content of your product catalog (i.e. product title, description, features) is, an evaluation is finished. If this content matches the search terms or keywords searched with the help of content users, it indicates the listing on the Pinnacle effect.

Now, the better the textual content relevance, the higher the ranking. This aspect makes it exceptionally necessary for you to optimize your listing. Creative titles, keyword-rich content, enticing descriptions, and clear bullet points rank the checklist at the top.

2. Sales Velocity

This is another important issue that the A9 algorithm considers when determining product rankings. Amazon defines this as the greenback volume and volume of a seller's transaction that has occurred at a stage in a month.

When estimating the velocity of income, it compares the seller's speed with its opponents for the actual search phrases typed by the user. The seller wins out with the right sales velocity.

3. Stock Availability

You may have heard many professionals insisting on having their item in stock. Ever questioned why? Well, an important point is that the algorithm is taken into consideration when indexing. If it says - out of inventory - be aware of that, your record is by no means going to top it.

Amazon does not want to pass out on a sale. If your product goes out of stock, you are disappointing your customers and this is something that Amazon no longer likes.

4. Price

In addition to displaying top-selling and relevant products, the A9 algorithm additionally tests whether the product has a suitable price. However, this section may be a bit elaborate due to the fact that A9 now not only looks at the quality charge but also looks at how the record has been properly represented. Therefore, try to balance these aspects.

Although the factors listed above are the largest for the A9 algorithm when assessing your product listings, some other elements do (but indirectly) perform an important function in addition:

5. FBA (Filled by Amazon)

The FBA (supplied with Amazon support) is one of the most valuable assets for sellers. When you've stocked your products in any of Amazon's warehouses, it helps you gain the fame of a "featured" merchant, handing you over to Amazon Prime members.

This additionally increases your chance of winning the buy box. Together, these gains led to a much larger path towards increasing sales velocity and conversions.

6. Advertising

Sales velocity is but the most important problem that appears for Amazon's A9 search algorithm. But the query on how to increase your income velocity? Well, the answer is through "advertising". Even the few greenbacks left for advertising can do a great job of getting site visitors to ride your product list. And if the product is staggered enough, then you have to generate more sales.

7. Customer Review

Undoubtedly, valuations play an important role in increasing universal sales. Positive scores and reviews from customers help the A9 algorithm identify whether customers are positively attractive or not.

To get ahead in this part, create an amazing client ride for site visitors searching through your listings. Strive for favorable and desirable evaluations to try and minimize poor response.

8. Images (High Quality)

In an online marketplace where consumers cannot physically interact with the product, photos are really everything. Bright, clear, and high-quality images of Amazon's "Zoom" feature product increase conversion rates. Upload as complete images taken in all angles, as it appeals to the A9 algorithm to boost rankings.

Amazon recommends staying at least 1280 pixels the longest. Ideally, you should go for ultra-HD snapshots, with 2560 pixels (or more) on the longest side.

9. Publicity

Yet other enjoyable ways to boost income momentum and increase conversions are through promotions. Although a phrase of caution. Consolidating your product can increase sales rapidly, although this is not a long-term way to increase your ranking. There are many more important, extra durable "A9" factors to focus on - such as your text's healthy relevance and product availability.

10. Premium Content

Using A + content (Vendor Central) and great brand content (Vendor Central) results in a 5% assist in sales. Premium content gives shoppers a better understanding of the product, often in lower returns and higher consumer satisfaction.

Elements of Amazon Product Listing

Talking about Amazon product listings, there are 6 factors associated with this. Be it personal labels or retail intermediation, these aspects are important to understand as a seller:

- Product image
- Product title
- Product Description
- Product features

- Product rating
- product reviews

  Be sure to follow the tips for each component related to your product listing, as well as through customization and enhancement to convert it. It helps you outwit your competitors, add value and expand your customer base.

  But what we did first?

  To create a high-quality product list, you need to analyze from top sellers. At SellerApp, we knew that there should be a fundamental difference between a well-optimized checklist and top-performing listings.

  With our set of tools, we can now not only detect them but will also provide an explanation for important tricks to improve your ranking.

  So, this is what we did. We took a product checklist from Amazon and analyzed how and why it performed so well. We analyzed this:

- Listing Quality
- Keywords Used
- The way the product was once described
- Number of reviews and ratings
- Whether it was completed by using amazon

Therefore, here are the effects that we have seen in every element:

1. Product Image

Of course, your product pics need to be clear, of high quality, and super to help you change. But the question is, how many pictures do you include?

You can best consider your images with the following criteria:

Close-up and clear images of images

Images must not be blurred

The product must be properly lit and have good concentrate

The product must be without recognizable problems

The product must occupy 80% of the area provided

In addition to presenting the best images, it consists of as many photographs as possible. Also, note that many product categories make you consist of swatches and optional images. Although Amazon allows you to add 9 images, we recommend you stay around 5 - 6.

Make sure the original photos are on a clear, white background. However, for others, history can be simple and simple.

2. Product Title

A product record containing between 50 and 80+ characters normally states its location between 1000 products. Now, this is actually the ability that your list contains at least eighty characters.

This is exactly what this record has done.

Note that Amazon cuts each product record to 112 characters. Therefore, it is mandatory to take some time to work on titles as this is one of the fundamental factors that determine their CTR (click-through rate) on the impact page.

3. Product Description

If a customer goes for your product description, they are more likely to buy your product, although still not positive.

Try to explain to consumers how your product can make a difference in their everyday lives and why it is necessary to buy it from you as an option compared to your competitors.

Considering the sample example, here is what they did with your product description.

Keep these suggestions in mind:

Keep details accurate, clear and concise

Include only data that relates to your product

Now don't use cost or testimonials here

We recommend keeping it 250 words minimum. But it is not too long.

4. Product Features

This is because paragraphs are bullet marks simpler and easier to read than a lot of texts.

Upon doing the analysis, we also found that most of Amazon's top sellers not only use bullet points to write the features of their product but also do not overdo it. They are not more than 5 bullet points.

The bullet point should include every important feature that is different from your competitors. Keep enough to make it interesting and reassuring for the buyer to shop.

5. Product Rating

Reviews of a product have a direct impact on ratings. They hold each other's hands. So, the higher the review, the higher the rating.

The listing below has a 4.3 out of 5 rating, which is certainly a good score but still has room for improvement.

The same has happened with this listing. You can see a highlighted button that reads - How to improve.

Now, if you are in the range of 4-5 stars, it means that you are doing really well. However, if your product struggles and has a low rating, here's what you can do to improve:

See patterns in bad or negative reviews.

Save and balance as many reviews as possible so that you can have a good rating and overall review.

6. Product Review

A successful product list consists of between 500 and 1000 reviews. No wonder this product list is generating a good amount of sales on a daily basis.

If a shopper is ready to buy your product, your reviews have the ability to influence them to make a purchase. Therefore, the higher the review, the better.

You can try running automated email services or use Amazon's reviewer program to collect some initial reviews.

You can search on Amazon's list or "Create a new product list".

Select a product category and subcategory to classify the item you sell.

You have to fill the details in each tab named Variations, Proposals, Pictures, Description, Keywords, etc. If you see the red warning symbol on any of these tabs, it indicates that you have missed entering the required details. Make listings available on Amazon Marketplace. Your list will not be published until you do so.

If you still encounter problems publishing the product list, you can always contact the Amazon seller support team at the top of the page, clicking the link - "Help" on the right. Follow the steps required to get help for the problem.

Amazon Product Video Guidelines

If you have shopped on Amazon, you may have come up with products that include a video about their product. This is a really smart move and one of the best ways to convince a buyer to buy your product, seeing that it is good enough and resolves the day-to-day issue.

Product cataloging with videos has a higher conversion rate as shoppers find that videos help to better explain product benefits and features.

Product Highlighter Video: Such videos are completely clean, simple and faceted on the

Product Interpretive Video: This type of video is impeccable with engaging scripts excellent and explains the advantages of using the product.

Note: The option to add product videos is enabled for brand-registered vendors. However, no official announcement has been made yet. This option is currently available at Amazon Seller Central under the EBC (Enhanced Brand Content) menu:

- Make sure you own the copyright to the product video you are going to upload.
- A product video must be made with a highly outstanding resolution.
- Product videos are both in their standard YouTube orientation or with a 16: 9 aspect ratios.

- The product video should have a minimum decision of 1280 × 720, but the correct decision is 1920 × 1080.
- Product videos must be recorded with an RGB (red-green-blue) color profile with 300 dpi. However, 72 may be acceptable.
- Product videos may not contain certain brand logos. It has to be only one.
- You have used Apple PrRes, you have to change it before uploading.
- The video thumbnail photo must be in PNG or JPEG format.
- The product video cannot include your contact information.
- Product videos may not contain distributor or business enterprise or vendor details.
- Product videos may not contain your competitor's products.
- The product video may not imply that you are an authorized seller or that it has been purchased by fully approved resellers.
- Product video may not include product price.
- Product videos may not contain descriptive trading facts (such as sales, hot sales, inexpensive, etc.).
- Product videos may not contain time-sensitive information (such as hot this year, now on sale, new item this year, etc.).
- The product video may not contain time or transportation cost details.
- The product video may not include something that indicates it can be used for the rogue activity.
- Product videos may not include records about customer reviews.

- Product videos may not contain 0.33 party or editorial citations.
- Product videos may not contain warranty or assurance details.
- Product videos may not include a company logo that you do not create yourself.
- Product videos cannot contain links to any website other than Amazon.
- Product videos may not contain distorted or objectionable content.

Whatever the motive, it is imperative to preserve your listing to improve more sales.

When we talk about "adaptation", we emphasize two matters here:

Optimized with possible key phrases to help rank for search phrases searching for the buyer.

Optimized with the correct set of images, titles, and descriptions to generate increased conversion rates.

Now, what most dealers forget is the assumption behind Amazon's A9 algorithm. Even if you have a very good record that is well adapted to Amazon, if a consumer feels that "it's not good," he is not going to buy it. it's clear.

It is not just about a customized product list. It is also about the quality of your product; its features and what customers think about it. Everything has to come together to make you're listing a success.

When you say "optimization", it's not just about meeting high rankings on Amazon's search results. It is also about creating a better and rewarding product overall.

3 Key Strategies that Will Help You Succeed on Amazon

1. *Come Up with a Great and Quality Product*

2. *Optimize Your Amazon Product List*

   However, you can work on the customization part to increase your entry in the search results.

   These are the 4 factors that shoppers see in the first 30 seconds after reaching your product page:

- Product Image
- Product title
- Product price
- product reviews

   The rest is where the customization part comes from. If you hit these details correctly, you can easily convert 90% of users.

Now, before you can really get into "optimization", there is an important step you need to do, which is keyword research.

3- Do Keyword Research First

Although you have Google Keyword Planner, it is best to have a keyword tool that only tells what buyers are looking for on Amazon's search box.

Once you have decided which keywords you want to target, the next step is to optimize your list.

Amazon Product Listing Customization Checklist

Optimizing the listing involves working on each element we describe.:

1. Product Title

If it's customized and yet creative enough, it can quickly tell Amazon, buyers, and searchers exactly what you're selling.

There is a way to represent it.

Do:

- Include possible keywords in the title, but use dashes (-) or pipes (!) To break up the keywords. This improves readability and does not appear to be misleading.
- Use primary keywords or search terms involving long-tail variations.

- Include the product's USP (unique selling point).
- Do not exceed 200 characters for product titles.
- Write the number of numbers (2 and not "two")
- If the product is a multiplier. Mention the quantity. Examples: 15-pack, set of 5, etc.

Do not do:

- Capitalize all words in the title.
- Include specific details of your listing. Example: free shipping.
- Include subjective adjectives like "brilliant, terrible, great, etc."
- Use special characters or HTML tags.
- Include too much information.

2. Product Features

Do:

- Use only 5 bullet points. However, if writing a little is really important, increase it to 6, but not more than that.
- Include the words call-to-action in these points.
- Make sure that the first letter of each bullet point is capitalized.
- Include points that help differentiate your product from your competitors.
- Use some keywords. But don't just shake them. Should be sensible while reading.

Do not do:

- Use too many keywords unnecessarily.
- Use exclamation marks at 3-4 full stops.
- Use lots of bullet points.
- Use special characters or HTML tags.
- Bullet points include shipping or promotional information.
- Include time-sensitive or subjective comments such as "hot sales" or "great prices".
- Use words like "unique design, stand out from the crowd, etc."

3. Product Images

Do:

- Include logo, text or watermark on images.
- If the product is a multiplier, show several diagrams.
- Include background on the main image. But this is fine if you are doing it for another secondary image.

4.Product Description

A good, accurate, small and clear product description steals the deal. You need to be innovative enough to convince them that your product will solve the everyday problems that they are facing.

Although product descriptions are shown on the detail page, they also feed into Amazon's search results and various external search engine results.

Do:

- Keep it short, clear and precise.
- Provide descriptive and factual information.
- Highlight essential features.
- Capitalize the first letter of each sentence.
- When writing a new paragraph, give a page wreck.
- Check for grammatical and spelling errors.
- Include the company name, mannequin number, and collection, even if they are already used in the title.
- Include color, size, and compatibility information.

Do not do:

- Use time-sensitive or subjective phrases such as "hot-sales this year, amazing prices, etc."
- Include distribution or promotional information.
- Use HTML tags.
- Include email or net tack here.
- Use symbols or unique characters.

5. Search Term

The section - search terms - is only shown in the back-end of the listing. Yet there is a whole lot of discussion on this part, although it is not as complicated.

Do:

- Use various key phrases that you cannot use in the product title.
- Include a few different secondary search terms.

Do not do:

- Include keywords you have already used in the title.
- Use the manufacturer title once again here due to the fact that Amazon will choose it automatically.
- Use subjective words like "Now available, best, on sale, etc."
- Use the vendor name.
- Use the misspelling of the product or any other version.
- Include any element that causes misinterpretation of the product.

Chapter 9: Generate Your First Sale!

In my experience, I've been able to get my first few reviews on products using JumpSend, so I can't stress how essential this tool is to your long-term success.

It may seem counter-productive to deliver your goods at a cut-price but think of these first sales as shopping for critics as an option as a profit.

Initially getting the right reviews is indispensable for your long-term success as an Amazon seller.

Settle your First Deal

Next, you will want to choose the product category.

In my case, this product is very good in the "pet supplies" category.

You will also choose whether your product is loaded using Amazon.

If you are following this direction on a T, then you would like to select "Fulfillment through Amazon".

Don't worry about the "price after discount" area as we will come to that later.

Once you have selected the whole thing, click "Next".

The latter page protects your product inventory.

Select the "Automatic Inventory Protection On" option to positive.

This option protects you from one person on JumpSend shopping for your entire stock with a coupon.

I support setting your "limit order quantity" to 1 because our stock is low at the moment.

On the subsequent page, an amazing video Jumpsend offers you will tell you how to make a coupon.

The only thing I will have is that I recommend setting your coupon somewhere between 60% -80%.

When you have coupons created, revisit the first page and enter the "discount after price" on the right, mainly based on the percentage-off you set.

On this page, I suggest you select "Manually Approved Shoppers" because you want to wait four hours from the time you set your coupon code on Amazon

You will then want to choose a template to start your email campaign.

Personally, I use the "two review request" template and have had particularly respectful success with it.

This part is entirely up to you how you like to personalize your personal electronic mail follow-up campaign, so I did not go into a great deal of detail.

I would say that the templates are very well made, and you probably have to change a lot of the words inside them.

When you remove a template, on the next web page you have to choose your product at the top of the page.

After making some changes to the messages you like, click "Review Campaign" and then "Activate Campaign".

You would additionally like to make sure that the "Message active" button is selected for each message.

Some notes while writing you're follow up email:

Do not spam your customers because it will in all probability get you into trouble with Amazon;

Do not link them to any YouTube video;

Do not link them normally;

Be very cautious when sending cases such as snapshots of PDFs. Although I trust that it is not in opposition to Amazon's TOS to do so, I will proceed with caution.

Now that we have shipped our merchandise to Amazon, we have done our first promotion, and have established email compliance with the campaign, we will eventually enter the world of Amazon PPC.

Setting Up your First Amazon PPC Campaign

Amazon Sponsored Product Applications (or Amazon PPC) is a great way to get your product in front of customers when your product is first getting started.

The purpose is to ensure that your product is placed organically, although for now, running ads may provide some much-needed exposure to your goods.

It has been said that running a product on Amazon PPC can also help its natural ranking.

Go to your seller's dashboard and click "Campaign Manager" under "Ads".

Finally, choose "Automatic Targeting" as we'll desire Amazon to create keywords based totally on your product info.

These keywords will be handy beneath Campaign; Ad Group; Keywords; Get record after your advert has been running for a few days.

You can use these keywords to optimize your record and set up a manual marketing campaign as well.

On this page, provide your Ad Group to identify and click the "Select" button next to your product.

Once it's selected, set your default bid and then click "Save and finish" to be executed placing up your first campaign.

Just supply your campaign a few days to run and you ought to be capable to download your record underneath Campaign; Ad Group; Keywords; Get file to see what key phrases your product is displaying up for.

These first few sales are integral to getting both opinions and rankings on Amazon, so be certain to no longer solely strive these two methods out however also spread the word to pals and household on social media.

I just mentioned that Fulfillment through Amazon would be a high-quality option to cater to your products in all types, so explain how to work on Amazon FBA.

- Find a product you like promoting on Amazon.
- List products for sale on Amazon.
- Prepare your items for shipment.
  Box your items and ship them to the warehouse location that Amazon assigns for the duration of the recording process.
  At this point, your work is about to be completed with the product.

.

Upon verifying that the objects are correct, Amazon will activate your listing. Two is the ability that your seller's identity will appear on the relevant product element page, and your item will be easy to sell.

Amazon will store the object in its warehouses until a patron order it.

Your share is too low to sell Amazon's fees. Two each time they send an order to you, you'll get an email from Amazon every time.

Every 2 weeks you will receive a credit score in your financial institution account for those credits purchased for the first 2 weeks.

Essentially, you are responsible for finding gadgets to promote and get them on Amazon. We will talk about the discovery of goods to promote later in this guide.

What are the benefits of using fulfillment with the help of Amazon programs?

There are some major advantages to selling on Amazon using Fulfillment with the help of the Amazon program.

When you sell on Amazon using fulfillment through the Amazon program, your items are available for all these top transportation benefits. Customers of two capacities can get free two-day shipping on the gadgets you sell.

In addition to fast shipping, customers are additionally aware that items shipped via Prime will have the same return coverage as those items that are purchased themselves with the help of Amazon.com.

What is the ability that customers can be exceptionally confident that their goods will deliver exactly as described and when expected? Not in this match that their expectations are not met now, they will know that Amazon's client carrier will solve the problem for them.

Serious self-confidence in customers towards the program are 2 major benefits that will help promote your items faster.

The other main benefit that I will mention is that Amazon carries a heavy load when using Fulfillment with the help of the Amazon application when selling on Amazon. Two you are able to ship gadgets to Amazon in huge quantities, and they deal with receiving items to individual customers.

Order Your Own on Amazon (Merchant Complete)

I mentioned above that while promoting on Amazon there was some other option that you no longer need to use Fulfillment by Amazon. The different option is "merchant fulfillment" that you promote on Amazon.

It is the ability that you will retain the items you have for sale in your area and when an order arrives, you will ship the object without delaying the customer. There are instances when this makes sense, although the use of Fulfillment by Amazon 99% of the time would be a high choice.

When my commercial venture considers satisfying our own orders, at the end of Q4, when an item does not have time to list in the FBA warehouse and sold before the holidays. In this case, it sometimes realizes Amazon's move from ship to ship to enable customers to get their products before Christmas and realize the processing time that comes with it.

So "merchant fulfillment" is an option, although, for the rest of this post, we'll focus on Amazon sales using the FBA program.

Now that we have a way to see how technology works, we'll get information on how to set up your seller account, how much you have to pay for the items you sell, gadgets to sell How to search for, how to charge your item, how to get your items on Amazon FBA warehouses, and what you can expect if you have items for sale on Amazon Cannot be applied.

To start promoting on Amazon, you want to register for an Amazon seller's account - this is different from your normal Amazon account that you use to buy goods.

This field will run you through the system of registration for an account:

- Step 1: Go to services.amazon.com.

If you click on the big "Start selling" button, you will start the registration process for a specialist account.

As the hyperlink means, you will get an individual seller account.

- Step 2: Choose between a personal and a business account.

When each choice requires additional fees, promoting your gadget incurs a $ 0.99 per item charge to the individual account that is not a blanket on the business plan. So, selling 40+ items to a robot in a month makes the business account a high deal.

The big difference is that to get the "Buy Box" you must have a professional account.

You can study more about which classes require approval and which ones are not through viewing this page on Amazon.

So, to remodel a professional account:

- It costs $ 39.99 a month.
- Removes $ 0.99 per item sales fee.
- The Buy box unlocks the ability to earn.
- Unlocks the ability to follow to promote in more categories.
- In the long run, it would without a doubt be a professional account.

This is to start with a personal account if you do not favor spending $ 39.99 and wish to check it out, but keep in mind that not being able to get the Buy box will restrict your sales as always, starting now is better than waiting, even if it means not getting a business account yet.

A lot of humans see the "legal name" field and hope that they want an LLC or some different inclusion position. Something I recommend when acquiring an LLC, you are flawed satisfactory for entering your personal full identity over time.

While it may only be a temptation to test that area and keep going, I am virtually taking the time to study the document. Yes, it is long and boring. This is additionally important.

Once you do this, you will be asked for your address, show name, and phone number. They will also ask you for a website, but you do not want anyone and can leave it empty:

Next, you want to fill out some financial institution accounts and tax information, and then ideally this is - you officially have an Amazon sales account. In unusual instances, you will get a message that they no longer want to issue you an account or want similar information. This is essential for the data you provide - meaning that your identification and handling are similar to the entire application and the types you submit.

It is a free app that is once accessible through Amazon which provides you with small prints like the selling price of the product, the fee and the different key points for any product that is on their website. The application is synced to your account without delay.

To locate a product, you can search for it through identification or UPC, or you can use a digital camera on your cell phone to scan the product's barcode. After this app will show you the pricing and charge statistics for that product.

This ability to scan products will be of great use when doing retail arbitration to collect products.

If you haven't yet set up a seller's account and favor looking at the profitability of an item, you can use Fulfillment using the Amazon Revenue Calculator to get rate critical points on any item Are.

If you go to fulfillment via the Amazon revenue calculator, promoting on Amazon. You will then enter the rate (red arrow), how much it will charge you to ship on Amazon (black arrow), and how many tons (green arrow) the product will give you. Two calculators will show you how much fees you will be charged, and the most important thing is how good income you can get to actually make it on that item.

I recommend that you sell every single object sold on Amazon through this calculator or a similar tool that serves the same purpose. With two calculators available like this, you know exactly how much you can earn on each item you promote on Amazon.

Now that we have a device that indicates to us how the price size works when selling on Amazon, we want some items to sell.

Search for Products to Sell on Amazon

The three most important approaches are to find goods to promote on Amazon. They are:

- Retail arbitration
- Bulk
- Produced your personal merchandise

These are all strategies for selling new items. When you can sell used gadgets on Amazon, most buyers use it to buy new items and I have had more success selling used items on eBay or local markets.

Wholesale sales involve partnering with existing brands and their distributors to get bulk orders to sell their products. Private labeling includes goods manufactured with their very own manufacturer on them.

The major attraction of these techniques is the conceivable returns and minimum time requirements once fully set and run. The trouble with these techniques is that they take too much ride and capital, to begin with.

So, while I recognize that it makes sense to use these strategies, I think it gives a lot of extra meaning to retail, to begin with, and as long as you find the travel and capital necessary, Do your work on them.

There is no obstacle to success with retail arbitration other than financing your time. If you are willing to do this, retail arbitration provides a clear direction to develop the ride and capital needed for wholesale, which in flip prepares you to be your own manufacturer.

When others tell you that you have already missed out on top-notch techniques and it will get easier, doubt it!

How to Get Started with Retail Arbitrage

To recap quickly, retail arbitration is one of the first-rate methods to start promoting on Amazon, as the initial money is low, it allows you to analyze the process, and has to have a good deal of cash.

The trip won retail arbitrage, as well as huge information on how Amazon's work could be promoted, which could be used for various inventory sourcing methods in the future.

To get started with Retail Arbitrage, you need to set up your seller account so that you can get access to the Amazon seller app. As mentioned above, it will present you with the records you need to see if an item is worth purchasing for resale.

Two-Income Rank is a piece of statistics that Amazon likes that gives us an idea of how fast an item is currently promoting on Amazon.

A complete dialogue of sales rank is beyond the scope of this post, although it is necessary to better identify the number of shortages. For your first few visits, I'm looking for sales ranks that are under 250,000. Two As you gain more ride, you can seriously tweak it, but rank below this range is a proper starting point.

If the app indicates that you are eligible to sell the item, and the rank is far below your threshold, then you desire to try and see if the item will provide a favorable return on investment.

You will be able to enter Amazon (I use $ 0.50 / lb.) promotion price, your price per pound and how many tons of items you can buy. Two in this example, I am showing that I can buy this item for $ 10.

At this stage, there are 2 quick exams you want to pass. The two first is to see if the internet earning number shown on the backside exceeds your minimum profit limit. Usually, I suggest keeping it around $ 3 per unit. This means that you have not purchased any item on which you will earn much less than $ 3 in earnings. Having a workable net income of less than two per unit of $ 3 can no longer make a lot of profit and a small drop in price can erode your profit.

If the item meets your minimum profit limit, you will want to calculate the return on money percentage. Two You can do this by dividing the net income with the help of the cost of the item. In this case, it is $ 7.13 divided using $ 10, so the return on the investment share is 71.3%.

When you are first starting to promote on Amazon, I am looking for an item with a return on investment percentage that exceeds 50%.

So, this particular item meets all the standards for purchasing the item and it is purchased. For any item that matches all purchase guidelines, I recommend purchasing up to 6 of the items.

Then it is time to repeat this process later on the item, and the remaining items are in the clearance section. Two When you are first getting started, I support scanning as many objects as possible. As you gain more experience, you will probably be able to keep away from scanning certain gadgets that will not appear attainable for resale. Two When first starting out, I recommend scanning as many objects as possible.

I support the technique of finding out that if an item is obtainable for resale in the order mentioned, you can rapidly pass on a subsequent item for any item that does not match your Before long, you'll find an item that matches your recommendations and you're eligible to sell - and you'll have the first item to sell formally!

Once you start searching for products, the perfect way to make positive what you find extra is by joining our BSL Speak Group. It is a group dedicated to sharing profitable retail intermediation with each other, including specialty products, stores, and profitability.

All individuals are required to share at least one qualifying deal each month, so you should have a good draw on how to search for products on your own before joining. Once you do this, this team is a great way to get a greater amount of merchandise each time you go sourcing.

How do I charge the items I'm selling on Amazon?

Now, we have some gadgets that we are in favor of selling on Amazon, we want to identify how to price them. Two When promoting the use of Fulfillment by Amazon program on Amazon, I suggest pricing at the same level as other Fulfillment through Amazon sellers on the listing.

To come to this screen, see All on-hand for the product. This can be accomplished by clicking on a hyperlink that says "used and new (#)" that will display just about every product for sale on Amazon.

I propose pricing between $ 41 and $ 41.41 if you are looking for a fast sale.

When pricing your items, I no longer advocate pricing under the prices you are competing with. The two pricing regulars in your opposition can initiate a chain reaction of lowering fees and quickly reducing margins.

On the extra aggressive side, I recommend matching the minimum rate of the same fulfillment method.

On the extra conservative side, I charge more than the lowest fee of the same achievement method between $ 0.01 and 1%.

As an aspect, if you are willing to wait for the item to sell, I would charge the item between $ 46.52 and $ 49.95 in this example. The motive for this is the somewhat different "gaps" that these gadgets are promoting. Two Whenever I am pricing an item, I will search for enough gaps in between offers, and if there is a good difference.

Listing your goods for sale and having them delivered to Amazon warehouses is your first step when you get your first products.

This step overwhelms many people, although it is actually very convenient once achieved.

This post will train you in everything you want to do when you have sourced your first products and are equipped to ship them to the FBA. It is usually less difficult to observe that you have a product that you include in the list, so I have stored this fact in a separate Book Instead of this post.

Starting Your Business

It has been too long - if you are stuck around and read it all, it is clear to me that you have an intense desire and motivation to start a business.

Whatever wants to inspire you for this change, I would like to motivate you to commit to action as quickly as possible. A put-up reading is no longer enough. It is not enough to plan to pick up some goods later.

Achieving the growth, you are making after the exchange - and the first element you want to trade is your own habits. Don't relax - doing this will pave the way to stay in the same place where you are now or a year old.

The excellent next step is to see the free presentation that I mentioned earlier on 7 keys. Determine commercial ventures for building 7 where you will study more about 7 figures and the rest of the techniques about stairway the ones I'm using to continue.

The course ahead is simple (if you will let it happen) but challenging (because it takes a lot of time and effort). There is no proper purpose to widen it either - I have already traveled the road you have been fascinated with.

Once you do this, there is a range of different coaching programs and offerings that I offer, like the BSL Bolo Team and Online Retail Pro, an intensive course where I share each final tip and strategy, which I'd like to introduce.

These are excellent ways to grow your commercial enterprise faster and bigger, but the most important factor is that you start. Depending on your situation, following the instructions in this guide, or enrolling in better education and coaching, you can also offer suggestions on the flipping challenge - but the most essential aspect is not how to get started, this is how you start in the first place. If you do this and are committed to succeeding, then it is a habit to fall completely in place.

During this post, we have covered everything it takes to start selling on Amazon. I want to close with a few tips and ideas that I think can help you based on the journey I had before.

The first factor I would say is that if the promotion on Amazon is right for you, then commit to giving it a shot as soon as possible.

You can examine retail arbitrage strategies that are put into it within a few hours and can be eye-opening through this method. Some humans like it and others cannot tolerate it. Two if you dedicate a few hours to it, you will recognize how you personally respond.

There is no reason to try this week.

The other primary aspect that I would say is to establish sensible expectations. The effort may just pay off.

Hopefully, this put has answered most of your questions about how to sell on Amazon and you have a better idea of what it means to sell on Amazon. Although this deposit is very broad, it is possible that you may have more questions. two

Chapter 10: Motivation and Successful Mindset

The Duty of Thought Turns into an Act of Self-Motivation

This can be an enterprise for many people, especially when the ride is new and the entrepreneur is working in the enterprise rather than working on it. Any lack of self-discipline and company can affect non-public reform and family, who routinely put on previously returned burners.

1. Set a personal mission statement

Every enterprise should have a mission or an imaginative and presentable statement, something that describes the organization's broader goals, way of life, and underlying core values. It is specifically used to determine the path of the agency and encourage stakeholders. For these same reasons, every entrepreneur should set out their own personal mission statement.

2. Make a plan

As with business, a mission assertion without a design to execute it is meaningless. You enhance and write your non-public and expert plan, which includes short time periods and long-term goals. This plan should not happen now and should not be panic and implicated, as it is organic and your non-public and business circumstances will change. That is the purpose, in my opinion, what you will achieve and how to achieve it. two

3. Start with a routine

It is about starting to excite yourself. For this reason, you should start each day with a morning routine, which will help your thinking and physique to be alert, targeted and organized to create new habits. Every morning as a part of your activities, you should spend time reviewing and refining your plan, or what John Mayer refers to as your eight for the day's routine.

4. Set time for yourself

Because entrepreneurs can often get completely stuck in their business, it is necessary to schedule non-public time throughout the day for themselves. During this time, allow your own flexibility to walk, think and meditate or exercise.

5. Plan ahead and set reminders

For this reason, reinforce a dependency to have reminders at some stage in the day for the necessary duties and daily wishes you set. Use your alarm, with a manageable volume, in addition, to remind yourself to be targeted at the task

You can also persist in using tracking techniques to keep unique periods of time in your calendar for precise tasks, initiatives or tasks.

6. Set the award

We are naturally starred in reacting to encouragement, so be prepared to reward yourself for accomplishing a purpose or maintaining a habit. Just like in business, you must recognize and reward long-term, broad goals as well as small wins.

And, if you need more encouragement, think about a clock that counts the rest of your lifestyle and reminds you what time you have left.

7. Enjoy friends

Sometimes peer pressure provides great inspiration. Engage your friends and colleagues to help inspire them towards personal and shared goals. Consider cellular apps that make engagement fun, such as Make Me, ChallengedApp, ClashApp, or of course text content for your partner.

8. Engaging in inspirational activities

Sometimes, you need to appear outside your circle for inspiration. When this happens, re-match a film you've considered inspiring. During your lunch break, watch a TED conversation. Or listen to an inspirational podcast throughout your day, taking a walk each day or when you are attending your personal time alone.

9. Stay positive

No one-size-fits-all answer is to please humans with definitions, principles, and opinions. For me, I have an easy mantra that I need to promote. It is simply, "Choose happily." Saying that with an idiom and a proper smile, I get to know my temperament and accelerate inspiration.

10. Sleep

Finally, don't underestimate a peak nighttime sleep for personal inspiration by any means. After years of travel and self-experimentation, I have determined that, with few exceptions, no incomplete challenge or unseen intention is worth the misery that comes with losing sleep over it. More importantly, with a clean night of rest, these tasks and goals become infinitely less complicated to finish the next day.

When your enterprise operates online, losing steam at a forward pace is clearly simple. Your competition, peers, and even your products exist in a digital environment - and there are no longer consistently tangible results for your challenging work. Because of this, motivation and motivation can sometimes come with help. Here are some tips for professional online commercial ventures, which keep you excited when excited.

Remember What You Are Working For

Even though on-line entrepreneurship can vary at times, for some business owners, it is all about focusing on the product and leaving the result. When productivity and motivation take off, why do they remind themselves behind their businesses?

Stan Farrell of ComposiMold says that for him, being excited is really about remembering what he's working for - and creating a product in which he can be just as perfect when you Working hard to believe something. Working long hours to make decisions is not always an exchange," he said.

Be Grateful for The Freedom and Flexibility

Ellie and Mac's Lindsay Esri said that the owner of an online commercial venture allowed her home to do a terrific job. "The owner of online business has forced my family (with four children) to travel the world," she said. "We have had such wonderful experiences because of it."

No one has the luxury of raising their personal program and performing as an owner - but on-line commercial enterprise owners do. Taking advantage of that flexibility is an accurate way to re-charge your new batteries.

Celebrate Your Freedom

Owning a commercial enterprise comes with a lot of risks, but it additionally helps the business proprietors to become self-sufficient and fiercely independent. In those days when you experience very less than motivated, keep in mind that your career direction allows you to choose your own adventures and challenges.

Erin Mulkeran said for me, "For me, this path has consistently intended that I have the possibility to create my own personal curriculum and make my own decisions. As long as I'm ready to work, I can call the shots. " Love Design.

Refocus

"I recognize that on-line entrepreneurship is about your survival and responsibility to participate actively in the community. If you can't do that now, it's time to re-think the business."

One of the great cases about being an online business owner is your ability to quickly shift gears and pass operations in a new direction. If you are no longer motivated, consider refocusing your business in a way that is better suited to your modern interests.

Early organizations hate the phrase and online marketing can be even more challenging. As there are web sites and competing agencies interested in just about every area of the imagination, using advertising can be an excellent challenge to stand out from your friends from the line. This is mainly if you do not have a good deal of cash to put into your advertising and marketing budget.

But there are a lot of recommendations that any on-line commercial enterprise can use to market their commercial venture, not missing their financial position.

Chapter 11: Tips for Your Online Business

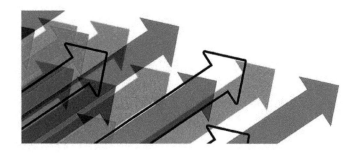

Tips to Improve a Profitable On-Line Advertising Strategy

1. Do not ignore your audience

This is the easiest, but most important tip of all, as market research is an integral part of marketing. Is there an exact demographic you are trying to attract?

A few open, appropriately open questions and then your personal market research habits. Be social and ask customers for their views and test what humans are saying about your company on social media.

2. Look into content marketing

You can take a humanitarian approach that points to your commercial enterprise as being a warm and pleasant place or talk about the ins and outs of the industry in a more technical fashion. As mentioned above, you need to know what your focused audience is and then create content that will cater to them.

Content advertising and marketing are extra cheap compared to general advertising, but it is challenging. You'll want to replace your content regularly. If you are involved in gaining additional knowledge about content marketing, then the Content Marketing Institute is an excellent place to start.

3. Get live on social media

Even if you publish the biggest blog ever, it is not counted if one does not read for sure. although it should tie content material advertising to a social media marketing campaign to reach workable readers.

But an energetic social media strategy no longer suggests developing a business account on every social media website. Focus on one of the most important social websites and gradually reveal yourself to others, once you are dependent on your first website.

You can also download the free model of MonsterInsights. It works great, but you won't get an entry for some of its best features.

Social media systems have exceptionally high audience participation. Facebook itself has 1.47 billion daily energetic users, which is about 18% of all humans in the world. Twitter, YouTube, LinkedIn, and other social media structures have specifically connected users.

With so many users, social media platforms provide great opportunities for business. You can start by increasing the social media profile of your business and automatically sharing your weblog posts.

- Create a Facebook team for your customers or industry
- Create a LinkedIn group for your industry
- Learn to Rebuild Customers on Facebook with Ads

  Focus on social networks important to your industry. For example, if you run a fashion weblog or restaurant, you may consider Instagram more useful than LinkedIn.

  Don't just send traffic to your website, use social media to build your email list;

  Do not spam these boards with links to your internet site in every post. Build authority, without doubt, collaborating with useful content, and refer to your enterprise or internet site when appropriate.

  Do you know that more than 70% of the humans who visit your website will never find it again? It's not your fault, it's just that the web is so vast and there are so many websites.

Every visitor who leaves your internet site is a receivable consumer you are missing. To develop your business, you need a focal point to convert those visitors into paying customers.

This is where OptinMonster comes in. It is the best conversion optimization software program in the market, which allows you to convert informal internet site traffic into loyal customers.

How does it do that?

It comes with a drag and drops campaign builder, where you can get personalized emails, display specific offers, exit-intense-up popups, countdown timers, smart popups, slide-in options, and more. It can create campaigns.

For more details, see this beginner's information on conversion charge optimization.

Affiliate advertising is a referral arrangement in which the online retailer (advertisers) will pay a fee to a referral when customers purchase a product using their referral link.

You want an affiliate administration gadget to affiliate the referral effort and will pay your affiliate partners. Here is our list of excellent affiliate management and tracking software that you can use.

You can promote products or offerings of various people to earn extra money from your content. See our affiliate advertising guide for recommendations and tools you will need to get started.

You can use these credits to test with PPC advertising and get some paid site visitors to your internet site for free.

Increase your Conversion

There is a list of sensible approaches to using social proof on your internet site to increase conversions:

-Use FOMO Effectively to Boost Sales and Conversions;

FOMO or 'fear of not being out' is a psychological term used to describe anxiety about something lacking in something exciting and fashionable.

Back in the ancient days, if you wanted to start your own business, you should have money impregnable so that you could open a storefront or lease an office to work. Thankfully, it was by no means less complicated to start an online business. However, just because it is so simple does not mean that you have to jump into anything before it is ready. Make the most of your new venture. The trap is an important ocean of possibility, so now is the best time to dive in and make waves.

-Know Your Competition;

This is a step that many new corporations fail before starting. Unfortunately, it is additionally an essential fact that it can help determine how you proceed and stay away from failure. Overall, your first step is not only to find out what kind of on-line commercial venture you desire, although how you can make it work as opposed to the competition.

When you look at your rivals, you like to pay attention to both influencers and younger people. Although you are not immediately competing with heavy companies, it is accurate to constantly see if that makes them higher than anyone else. What does their website look like?

-Social Media;

Although a brand's website tells you how they work, don't forget to pay attention to their social media and advertising outreach. Look at the systems they interact with the most and see what people are announcing about them. Look at them as a hashtag on Twitter for how regularly they are mentioned, and how high they pay interest for quality or negative responses.

Overall, this is the intention of the parents, what you can offer your competitors. You desire to discover their strengths and weaknesses, so you know what to keep in mind with your customers and what to pay more attention to. Take advantage of their knowledge and understanding and guide you to success.

-Protect your Brand's Online Reputation;

Since your company exists online, you need to make sure that your website reflects the best components of your online business. If it seems hard, customers will run away. Overall, you take these key elements into consideration to ensure that your web site works properly for your brand.

Maintain Consistency: If your web page is heavily modified between tabs, it will annoy and annoy your customers, to make them jump.

Follow standard formatting: It has a symbol on the left side that usually has a home page. Also remember that the information above the fold (above the screen) is the most valuable, seeing that most people do not like to scroll.

Unless you are well versed in website layout and programming, it is much better for you to hire a specialist to handle the entirety.

-Maintain a High-Quality Mailing List;

When you first start, building a neighborhood is fairly straightforward due to the fact that not many customers interact with it. As you grow and become extra popular, it then also becomes an additional quintessence to pursue and curate an energetic mailing list.

First, you favor presenting contact information for your business to humans. Email addresses are all you need, even if cellphone numbers can allow you to communicate in SMS marketing, which is every other valuable tool.

Calls to speed up your social media and internet site will help lead in new leads and generate a more comprehensive mailing list. You choose your CTA to be bold and be attractive in addition to being very attractive. There is a high responsibility to ensure that there is a technique to let customers know that they get a discount through membership or exceptional entry to new content material.

When acquiring your customers, it is fundamental that you create a personal message. Again, humans want to have a sense of respect, which cannot happen when there are sections of a 3000-person email blast. Two If possible, categorize your mailing list based on every customer's wish and customize the messages for each category.

-Be Independent Before You Ask for Money;

Unfortunately, getting into debt is very easy for most businesses. One of the reasons for having loans with new businesses is that they do not understand how theology wanted to start as a whole, or they try to grow before they are ready. Thankfully, on-line organizations do not require a ton of capital to start.

As far as development or development is concerned, you want to make positive that you are not reducing your popularity anymore. Do not hoist the gun just because your internet site visitors have increased. Instead, wait until you already have a well-established base until you start getting painful about doing more.

Given how terrible time and effort you have to put into your new company, this should be something you love to do, not just a capability. If your essential intention is financially motivated, then it will feel like a complete job. As a result, you will start to get annoyed at how big a "job" you have to do, which will either outsource things to you to different people (which will give value for money) or provide them altogether.

Instead, start a commercial venture because it is your passion. If not, why are you including yourself in that situation?

Even though an online business is not always included as a good deal, sweat, and tears as a popular storefront, you still have a lot to put into the company. In the end, it will become your phase, so make positive that it is a part that you like, not one that you want to hate.

Useful Information to Know Before You Start

If you are thinking about using Amazon Achievement Services to manage your orders, here are various things you need to know before you start:

1. It Will Cost You

There is no round to it: when you use the FBA, you are about to spend cash.

The Amazon FBA charges marketers for both storage and supplies. You will actually be paying "rent" for the house that occupies your goods in Amazon's warehouse, as well as fees related to pleasant orders.

However, you will not pay a lump sum for delivery. Because the shipping price is considered part of the achievement fee and rolled into the FBA fee.

Although there is some true news. As an Amazon FBA seller, you are additionally eligible for the company's two-day delivery that Amazon Prime customers provide, which means Amazon's most loyal customers can order their products online and Can only hold it in two days without any extra. Fees to you or the customer.

Now, return to the Let's Go faculty and do a quick cost-benefit analysis of the Amazon FBA application

Benefits: FBA offers outsourced shipping, fine buyer service, and appeals to Amazon Prime participants with two-day shipping. If you are currently shipping yourself, you can issue with FBA as low in cost as retail time.

Costs: FBAs have hard costs that include storage and achievement products, which are on a sliding scale. The fees will be based on the measurement of your products, which you prefer to store in Amazon's warehouse, and how you regularly fulfill your orders.

Luckily, Amazon makes it easy for you to analyze your profits and expenses with FBA. See the company's price calculator.

The bottom line, however, is two that it is about the bottom line. Consider success with the help of Amazon fees as money in inventory management, operations, and marketing. You must determine whether the amount of FBA costs is worth the returns generated through sales on Amazon.

2. There Is No Sales Quota

You might assume that a company as large as Amazon would need to go to a certain amount of mark every month if you wanted to be a section of the FBA application, although this is not the case.

Amazon knows that not all goods are created equal now and demand for some gadgets is softer than others. The enterprise is more than fully satisfied to provide FBA services to small commercial enterprise owners who do not pass stock quickly.

With FBA, you can promote only a few products in a month or you can sell piles of goods each month.

3. FBA Is Not Mandatory

The top information for small groups is that we can all sell merchandise on Amazon in addition to using FBA.

Some marketers find that they can handle the total pick, pack, and ship process on their own for less cash than what it would cost to use Amazon's service.

Of course, they would additionally have to find a location to protect their products and manage buyer complaints and hassles associated with returns.

Again: Think of Amazon FBA as an investment. Selling your goods with the FBA will likely generate a good return on investment. On the different side, you should stand to make a lot of cash through handling success.

4. You Can Fulfill Orders through other Channels Using FBA

You will probably be under the impression that the FBA will only fulfill orders from the Amazon website, although this is not the case. You are not restricted to using FBA only for your listings on Amazon.

As you build your e-commerce business, you can find out that you appeal to customers from all over the world through your awesome consignment list on various websites. If so, then you should be aware that Amazon FBA will fulfill orders from these various sites as well.

The FBA can be a centralized shipping and customer provider operation center that will manage orders placed on any quantity of advertising channels around the world, regardless of where this order is placed.

5. You Still Have to Pay for Shipping to Amazon Fulfillment Centers

Although your shipping fee to customers is cooked at the FBA cost, you will need more than some cash to bring your products to the achievement center.

Therefore, technically, you are still working with a moderate amount of delivery cost.

However, Amazon has given the option to partner to allow sellers to ship products to Amazon's breakthrough features at a dramatically lower cost.

When you use Amazon-partnered carriers, the agency provides you with a transport label for the container that you are shipping to the warehouse. The cost is given in your FBA account as an "inbound transportation charge".

If you have a large quantity of merchandise that you would like to send to an achievement center, Amazon additionally offers a partial cargo and full truck loaded option. If you are in favor of using that service, you will usually need a dock or forklift.

6. There Is No Limit on Inbound Transportation to The Supply Center

Amazon does not state any minimum or most restrictions on how much of an achievement you ship in the middle of a shipment.

This is true news, especially when considering a higher transport price, to work with smaller, more standard shipments than with a huge shipment.

Luckily, as an Amazon FBA seller, you can feel as free as you can fit your product line in a single shipment.

7. Amazon Uses the FIFO Method to Determine Storage Fees

As we saw, Amazon has spent your goods to be stored in its warehouse, and these fees can be traded seasonally or depending on the quantity.

As a general enterprise owner, you are potentially curious about how Amazon will spend for storage space. It uses the first-in, first-out (FIFO) method.

In other words: Your first batch of products that arrive at the warehouse will also go out the door first when customers order them. Once they are gone, they will not be concerned about storage fees.

New items that come to change historically will be subject to storage fees until they are sold. You are potentially subject to various FBA charges if you ship to stock in the low-rate season and additional shipments in the high-rate season.

8. Amazon Charges Long-Term Storage Fees

If your inventory runs too slowly, you may be slapped with a long-term storage charge, in addition to other FBA achievement fees.

Items left in the warehouse for more than six months are issued for a long-term fee. If you have a commodity that is in very low demand, you will need to apply that component to your cost-benefit analysis.

You can use Amazon's Inventory Age and Inventory Health Report to identify the status of the long-term position of which items in your inventory.

9. *You Cannot Avoid The "Pick and Pack" Fee*

You would probably think that you could keep people on Amazon for some time - and yourself some money - through packing your merchandise as you would like it to be delivered to the customer.

Unfortunately, delivery requirements on Amazon make the "pick and pack" charge completely unavoidable. So do some shopping yourself and ship merchandise on Amazon in the easiest way.

10. *It is Best to Start Slow*

With many different cases in business, the first category is to start sluggishly with Amazon FBA.

This is due to the fact that you do not know what you do not know. Even after reading this observation, there will be constant unexpected costs and unexpected challenges. If you face those problems on a small scale then it is fantastic.

Start with the help of Amazon FBA to offer fully controlled products for sale. Give a shot for a few months.

After a few months have passed, consider your charges and income. Determine if you can make a lot more money by using a carrier for a larger component of your product.

If completeness is fine, then you can eventually centralize your transport functions with FBA.

11. Escrow Has Money from Sales

Once you ship your products to Amazon Warehouse and they go live on the site, customers can start ordering them; but you will not get paid right after each order.

The method looks like this: Amazon gives the consumer the price of the item and any related income taxes. Then, Amazon removed its shortfall from the sale and put the cash into escrow for a couple of weeks.

Money is saved in escrow in case of returning the product ordered by the customer. Patience becomes fundamental when working with Amazon FBA.

So, as with many different things in life, you have to wait for the Amazon FBA to come to you.

12. Amazon FBA Fees are in Addition to Commission

Remember: Your Amazon fulfillment and storage fees are in addition to your commission expenses and separate sales fees.

If you have decided to do a delivery deal on your own, you can still sell Amazon as a fee according to the ratio of your sales, regardless of the sales format you work on. That sales plan will not run simply because you use FBA.

13. *You Can Save Money by Creating Your Own FBA Shipping Plan*

When you ship your products to Amazon to complete, the business enterprise will find out which warehouse is right for your products.

After a while, Amazon may assume that it is a fair idea to move your merchandise to another warehouse.

Unfortunately, the seller is responsible for shipping costs when this occurs. Amazon does not rent cowl in the new warehouse.

You can avoid these unexpected costs and warehouse changes through inquiries for your personal delivery plan.

Of course, if you are in favor of increasing the high-quality transportation plan, then you will need to understand your target demographic and most of your orders will be shipped.

14. *Your FBA Account May Be Suspended*

When you promote on Amazon, you have to play according to the rules of the company. If you do not, you should lose your account.

In particular, here are some violations that will make you lose your promotion privileges on Amazon:

Having more than one vendor account - If you favor another account, you will need permission from Amazon.

Opinion manipulation or misstep - Amazon is cracking down on fake reviews these days. If you want to protect your account in a suitable condition, do not pose as part of the trouble through buying fake reviews.

Satisfactory Products - If there are enough human bitches about the high quality of your products, Amazon will pull the plug on your account.

Violating mental property legal guidelines - If you are going through the creative work of someone else as your personal and Amazon know, you can suspend your account.

Fulfillment through Amazon is a great way to hand over a lot of the hassles associated with e-commerce to a corporation with a fantastic online popularity.

However, you will pay a rate when you get Amazon's help. Make sure you calculate the fee and component it into your viable profit margin before joining Amazon FBA.

Conclusion

Thank for making it through to the end of *Amazon FBA for Beginners*, let's hope it was informative and able to provide you with all of the tools you need to achieve your goals whatever they may be.

In my opinion, FBA is a must-have provider for the products listed on Amazon. Being able to enable quick transportation (which is often free to the customer) is key to conversion on Amazon. Using Amazon's warehouses for your Amazon income means a lot.

For these dealers who are considering FBA as a delivery provider for their own online store, this is also a strong option. However, multi-channel vendors do not make as much profit as Amazon sellers. Before you decide on the FBA, you can take a look at Shipwire to evaluate the pricing.

Despite this, I look at any evaluation that says FBA is a sinister option. Most retailers find success with the service, mainly for products that are listed on Amazon.

When you are ready to learn more about Amazon FBA and how you can use it to benefit you and get you further in your own goals and dreams, make sure to read this guidebook to help you get the right tips and tricks to get started.

Finally, if you found this book useful in any way, a review is always appreciated!